I0437044

JUNG, FAUST
and the
DEVIL

Return to Alexandria &
The Voices of the Dead

Bernard X Bovasso

authorHOUSE®

AuthorHouse™
1663 Liberty Drive
Bloomington, IN 47403
www.authorhouse.com
Phone: 1-800-839-8640

© *2012 Bernard X Bovasso. All rights reserved.*

No part of this book may be reproduced, stored in a retrieval system, or transmitted by any means without the written permission of the author.

Published by AuthorHouse 8/9/2012

ISBN: 978-1-4772-1610-1 (hc)
ISBN: 978-1-4772-1612-5 (e)
ISBN: 978-1-4772-1611-8 (sc)

Library of Congress Control Number: 2012910661

Any people depicted in stock imagery provided by Thinkstock are models, and such images are being used for illustrative purposes only. Certain stock imagery © *Thinkstock.*

This book is printed on acid-free paper.

Because of the dynamic nature of the Internet, any web addresses or links contained in this book may have changed since publication and may no longer be valid. The views expressed in this work are solely those of the author and do not necessarily reflect the views of the publisher, and the publisher hereby disclaims any responsibility for them.

Sermio IV
The dead filled the place
Murmuring and said:
Tell us of gods and devils,
Accursed one!
The god-sun is the
Highest good;
The devil is the opposite.
Thus have ye two gods.
The Seven Sermios to the Dead written by Basilides in
Alexandria, the City where East toucheth the West.
C.G.Jung[1]

CONTENTS

PREFACE

Duplexity intends the State of Twoness whose peculiar reference is to the term Binarius, another name for what is designated in Biblical Scripture as the Devil or Satan. Otherwise personified it is familiar as the principle of Evil and is accounted for as the Second Day of Creation that ends on the Sixth Day as the creation of mortality. With mortality Death is posited so that The Binarius has close association with Hades, the Lord of Death and which implies the greatest Evil known to humans is Death and in extension, the abscence of Immortality or in any way what in The One before two is designated as God the Father.

At this point the ontological (Beingness) falls back on the numerical One and Two for the simple reason that they indicate alternate realities both in effect at the same time. Theological this is the problem of Good and Evil. Psychologically, however, it poses the question of choice, literally which of my duplexity of personality is either the favored or more active one, indicating that the choice in the matter dispatches the other one to unconsciousness. But this is equally the problem of Twoness and appropriately of the Devil's party since there hardly any freedom of choice for which Ones of the Two is to be favored. This was characteristic for the Swiss Analytical Psychologist, Prof. Dr. C.G. Jung of Zurick who made published claim in his memior of having two personalities. Because the life of Jung has enjoyed wide biographical and autobiographical exposure the problem of Twoness or, if you will, The Binarius, stimulates a universal concern for the work of the Devil as instrumental may be intended as either coming into being or not to be as the beginning of mortality and its consequence in all aspects of phenomena extending Old Nick as the agency of this and its other and the choice of either doing your duty or getting off the pot.

Bernard X Bovasso

INTRODUCTION

Jung and His Other

The name *Philemon* has reached public notice as much as the name of its author, Analytical Psychologist Prof. Dr. C.G. Jung. This is not so odd considering that more is publicly known about the man Jung on a multi-dimensional level than many a celebrity in recent history. Much has been revealed for all to see from the level of depth, breadth and intensity that not only includes his pioneer work in Depth Psychology but the more recent publication of his secretive creative endeavors now broadcast in a lavish facsimile edition of his original closet composed Red Book. As if suddenly the man of mind and his science of the psyche is brushed aside for the man of fabulous fantasy magic. That would be to say the man Jung has been eclipsed by his own imaginary man, Philemon.

Who is Philemon and by what power does he take stage center? Jung did not have to answer this question involving his successor because he insisted that the "all his life" closet work be made public only posthumously, almost as if to publicly reveal this other of his life as in fact a prognostication of his afterlife. Hardly a morbid preoccupation: the subject of Death and all that goes with it from the mythological to the metaphysical and theological filled his life from childhood on. However, this was only the secret and occluded Jung that voiced what he called his No. 2 personality. No.1 personality, by contrast was Jung up front as practicing Analytical Psychologist very much involved with defining the epistemic nature of the psyche and its individual and collective affectivity. My own interest in the man and his work is thus developed part in awe and part in critical assessment of him and his multidimensional, if only duplex approach to himself, the world and, of course his patients, family and friends.

PART ONE: THE BENARIUS PERSONALITY

Psychic Duplexity

But who or what is Philemon? I will take the liberty of suggesting that the etymology of the name is not so cryptic as Jung would prefer it, the better to further conceal this automagical fantasy Other: However the name was borrowed from Greek mythology its etymological construction is telling: "Philo," as in "brotherly love" and "Mon" combine to simply indicate "love of the One." Considering that Love is classically divided according to three affectations: Erotic Love, Brotherly or Platonic Love and love as Agappe or intense passion and rapture, The Mon as One would include all three forms of love. Not, however, to stop there when it may be noted that "Mon," as in "mono" is a close etymological cousin to the Greek *on* and *ontos* (being and beings). Checkpoint again by the good doctor: Philemon for all his dress with horns and wings represents ontology or what is the metaphysical cream of philosophical milk since the era of pre-Socratic Greek physiologoi, students of nature.

Here the question of The One lags since no sooner posited than the Other of One takes stage center. Jung voiced his ontological problem of the One and its Other by noting his two personalities he called "No. 1" and "No.2." Aside from his Other Worldly unus mundus concerns the man Jung set his own stage by indulging his two personalities, often as much in complaint as in awe of his own duplexity.

Attempting thereby this study, the man Jung and his Other as Philemon, had to be explored as they ranged between Jung No. 1, his given extraverted personality and its alternate destiny as his lurking No. two introversion where the image of Philemon serves his palingenesis. He notes:

> No. 2 had no definable character at all: he was *avita per-acta*, born living, dead, everything in one; a total vision of

1

life. Though pitilessly clear about himself, he was unable to express himself through the dense, dark medium of No. 1, though he longed to do so. When No. 2 predominated, No. 1 was contained and obliterated in him, just as, conversely, No. 1 regarded No. 2 as a region of inner darkness. No. 2 felt that any conceivable expression of himself would be like a stone thrown over the edge of the world, dropping soundlessly into infinite night.[2]

Was No. 2 his inferior man representing what Jung would call the "shadow" and by which he meant inferior because undeveloped? That would render it as archaic: the shadow man as the Devil, properly dwelled in the underworld of unknowing as the Lord of Death himself who reigns over "infinite night," From that standpoint "No. 2 regarded No, 1 as a difficult and thankless moral task, a lesson that had to be got through somehow, complicated by a variety of faults such as spells of laziness, despondency, depression, inept enthusiasm for ideas and things that nobody valued, liable to imaginary friendships, limited, prejudiced, stupid, (mathematics!), with a lack of understanding for other people, vague and confused in philosophical matters, neither an honest Christian nor anything else."[3]

Apparently the Devil was demeaning a distinct and in this world personality and numbering its deficiencies, yet in turn by inverse description that personality's potential. Would it be common to assume the Prince of Death and Evil as the agency forcing the No. 1, or Jung's given personality, to introspect by offering its deficiencies so concisely? In other words, it was the lord of Death that turned on for Jung a psychological, rather than a philosophical or theological principle. Thank the Devil then for advising what is descriptive of a confused young man to "heal thyself" much before he became a doctor. In this way No.1 pulled itself together and pursued a chosen career in psychology.

It must then be wondered why and how the Lord of "infinite night," Death & co., used its byline in Evil to such purpose except become aware that Death as without articulated definition, is a pleroma of oblivion and "nothingness," as it were: the Void precluded in time and space or in short what is comparable in description to the Biblical First Day of Creation. This also fits the description of what much, much later fascinated Jung in his interest in alchemy as the unus mundus, the transcendent One World or World of The One by whose power base metals could be transmuted into gold. But this would raise the question of whether The One and its world was of the Divine Father or his fallen Son as the Devil. On the other hand, the Devil was, in relation to God, also God's inferior self and more functionally charged with doing His "dirty work" in the matter of creation and Genesis. He is as such, not the immovable One but the first digit that begins the generation of numbers as strictly a No. 2. sort of fellow and, accordingly, known as the Binarius. If No. 2 is moralized, as Jung quickly does when he notes, "A thinker of the Middle Ages noticed that when God divided the upper waters from the lower waters on the second day of creation, he did not say it was good in the evening as he did on all the other days. God did not do so because on the second day he had created the Binarius."[4] Surprisingly, Jung as a psychologist failed to notice that no relation between Father and Son is "good" as would be the case for Oedipus who is also the diabolus (opponent) of the Father as are all sons insofar as their gender identity is dependant upon the father as a role model. Finding his identity as his own man the father imago must be disposed. Nevertheless, the archetypal animosity and diabolus friction is par for the course in such a relation and by no means a literal intent to "murder" the father and thus dispose of the original love between father and son. Yes, of course, in the neurotic situation "murder" is the first archaic thought. More likely, however, a father surpassed by his son is proud of him. God the Father and as *The One* thus only euphemistically does not overlook his blessing on his filial No.2 when in fact birthed him and allowing him to "Fall" from the heavenly womb of the unus mundus and which is the First Day of Creation. The idiotic moral indignation arises more likely because Number Two" is in the position of generation as demiourgos and thus in close association with the maternal function of "making" (poieia), the feminine realm which is No. 2 to No.1 who is her husband and father of the intermediate diabolus who serves the role of messenger, the same role played by Hermes in the Greek mythos. It may thus be said that the son has something of the Paraclete about him in his seminal function to the world (which is his mother and his Father's wife often referred to as Mother Israel and the Shikinah.

The primordial feminine as such would have an animus or a masculine spirit-form variously referred to as Hades, Satan, the Devil and Mephistopheles. Subsequently, as an animus figure The Devil is not only second best to its hostess, the unus mundus virgin womb place, but to his Master as God the Father. In that sense, The Devil as animus to the ur-mutter is as her animus representative, the Lord of Death, in this case as the oblivion indicated of the void and vacuous unus mundus. But as oblivion or lethe (the concealed) it is more likely a pleroma of nihilio, or simply "nothing," and stands in metaphor to a virgin womb or place, as Plato indicated in his Timaeus, as a substrate womb-like "receptacle" (Chora, *xwpa*) "without previous impress." Need it be added, accordingly, that the animus of this empty or virgin womb-space is also its Lord and Master as the Prince of Darkness and infinite night. It would thus follow that the Prince of chthonios has incest on his mind and would like to take his virgin mother to wife and in effect populate her barren unus mundus and which is no less why Jung, apparently without knowing it, was citing the voices of the dead in his "Seven Sermons to the Dead." In that sense the voices of the dead are seminal and why Hades is first represented as a phallus. I am not sure Jung cared to address this even, as he reports, he dreamed as much when three years old, of a giant icthyphallus rising up in an underground place: that all The Dead wanted was to be received in the infinite night of the unus mundus as persistent seminal intruders. On the way, some of this primordial intent to beget something new rubbed off on the young Jung to make something of his No. 1 personality. Hence, his childhood nemesis, Jesus qua the Devil, is in fact his helpmates representing his dormant personality No. 2. They are related as two brothers much in the manner of Jacob and Esau the latter of whom was known for his redness and wild nature, indeed the Devil in red recast as the inferior son, the fiery one that is Two! And so it was with Ishmael, the inferior or outcast son whose complement as his chosen brother, Isaac. In addition, if "Our Father who art in heaven" fathered two sons they would appear, accordingly: the one in redness as the Devil and the other the son in whiteness and luminous Revelation. Indeed one is the necessity of the other insofar as the son in redness was assigned the role of demiourgos and creator of the world and which from the outset in the Divine Garden required a redeemer for its sin of Being (in the image of the Father).

Uubermensch und Untermensch

Looking back to Nietzsche's definition in his *Ecce Homo*: "The word *Übermensch* [designates] a type of supreme achievement, as opposed to 'modern' men, 'good' men, Christians, and other nihilists ... When I whispered into the ears of some people that they were better off looking for a Caesar Borgia than a Parsifal, they did not believe their ears," and which

Nietzsche poetically carries to unpleasant extreme: *"Yes! I know whence I come!/Like a flame, unsatisfied/I glow and consume myself./All that I touch, turns to light,/All that I leave behind, is coal/Assuredly I am a flame."*

The expressed elitism of the necessarily inflated and heated up personality is, unfortunately, literally played out by those in theological, moral and personality correctness as pure in origin and race, where such a "flame" was equally demonstrated in the crematoriums of the concentration camp, ostensibly to clear the path for *Übermensch* of such inferior beings designated as Jews who would corrupt the "purity of Aryans." Using Nietzsche's metaphor, the Ubermensch would be flame and the light whereas the Jew as Untermensch would be the coal and what fuels such hubris. Here we have the brothers Satan and Jesus, Jacob and Esau, Isaac and Ishmael as each the adversary of the other but who are as much in love as father and son simply because as The Two they are of The One.

Was Jung's Philemon also his spirit fire, all light in the sense of knowing or all consuming heat in the cause of death and destruction? Indeed, Nietzsche did not have Parsival in mind and what "good men and Christians." savored. But, which way did Jung and his Philemon lean, considering that his wife Emma spent a good part of her life involved with the subject of the Holy Grail where Parsival's quest was perhaps her own. Was it her husband's as well, whether as his No. 1 or No. 2? Notably, the German composer Wagner queried the spelling of Parsifal instead of *Parzival* and which followed an erroneous etymology of the name Percival. However, turning good things sour from One to Two, the latter was derived from a supposedly Arabic origin, *Fal Parsi* meaning "pure fool!" Indeed, stand a good Parsivalian Christian on his head and, of course, you will find a *Fal Parsi* or the *untermensch* as the radical Muslim's "infidel," fit only for extermination. It is thus not an idle gesture that *Der Fuhrer* persuaded Persia to change its name to "Iran" which is but a slip of the tongue for "Aryan" and what has prevailed as the original nemesis of the Jews as those who would pollute the Aryan race by producing Soter and his brother in Twoness, duplexity and as Binarius or The Devil.

Aside from such extremes of collective inflation, was Jung, on the other hand, deceived by his own figment of the Spirit when he notes: "Philemon and other figures of my fantasies brought home to me the crucial insight that there are things in the psyche which I do not produce, but which produce themselves and have their own life. Philemon represented a force

5

that was not myself. In my fantasies, I held conversations with him, and he said things that I had not consciously thought. For I observed clearly that it was he who spoke, not I."[5] To whom or which of his two personalities was Jung listening, himself or an other that remained more or less unknown? He must then apologize by noting: "The play and counterplay between No.1 and No. 2, [personalities] which has run through my whole life, has nothing to do with a 'split' or dissociation in the ordinary medical sense. No.2 has been of prime importance, and I have always tried to make room for anything that wanted to come to me from within. Most people's conscious understanding is not sufficient to realize that he is also what they are."[6] "He" represents Jung's less conscious and subliminal No 2 introverted personality that seemed active when he was a child, but was hidden from his No. 1 and active personality that was a barrier to that which "wanted to come to me from within." Its complement, No.1, and foremost personality would indicate his conscious or active extraversion that served him during his early professional career and association with Freud during the early days of Psychoanalysis.

The Other: as Anima & Shadow

This "he" as *Other* and simultaneously "brother," however, had a less than comforting component. It first emerged for Jung as a small boy in his dream of a brazenly erect underground phallus. Its erotogenic residue was apparently unconsciously embedded in his adult extraverted No. 1 personality where it was glaringly active in his erotic necessity for a series of young mistresses who, in turn, were projections of his "inner woman" or anima. A young mistress qua anima, however, as his feminine soul principle, was not directly related to the giant underground phallus because its archaic nature was far too rooted as a nightmarish visitation beyond comprehension for anyone, nevermind a small boy.

Although Jung notices in his Memoir how this dream was subliminally retained all his life, he amplifies no further, as he might have if it were not so close to home as his own mother for whom such an obscene image was in fact an animus representation that could not be admitted in her consciousness but projected, and hence disposed of in her innocent boy-child animus that was the image's polar opposite. As a most archaic and rude animus image, it served the obscure relationship between mother and son that is archetypally fixed as an imperative of the child's development.

Jung does admit, however, his mother was quite awesome to him as a child, more so than his father whom he would soon enough displace in his own intellectual development. Not so the mother who had him doubled as a *conicidentia oppositorum* animus projection, that is as simultaneously the two in one of son and lover, in either case as Soter (savior) and Diabolus (adversary). But if what is so far developed as the primordial animus of the feminine psyche, namely the phallic Hermes, Hades and then the Christian Devil, rings true, then certainly the three year old boy was dreaming his mother's dream! The phenomenon of children dreaming for their parents, especially when a parental complex is involved, would not much later on be news for Jung except that the little mother lover was cast in the role of No. Two as second best to his father and mother's husband. This would cast the son in the role of a "little devil" intent on replacing her husband and thus prevailed as adversary of the father. The Devil as Satan, on the other hand, is also the "accuser" and carries the intent of the dead to accuse the living or, better say, remind them of their mortality and who will soon join the dead. Moreover, if they do not learn their role as dead they must go on wailing as the "voices of the dead from Alexandria where the Hellenic world joined with that of the Persian East But regardless East or West, the agency of Death bears representation as a serpent or, less shamelessly concealed, a Phallus where its seduction of Eve is wordless and her passion in silence.

Jung's dream of the chthonian icthyphallus thus did in fact anticipate much of Jung's "voices of the dead of Alexandria." What this tells us may be deadening for the deterministic nature of a masculine dominated society and its notion of male priority and sovereignty: that every boy lives out his mother's unconscious projected dream, and its psychic prognosis by which her animus takes its primordial form as the phallus as non other than her little devil of a son. In addition, need it be said, what man's wife is not chosen as a shade of his mother? In turn, the wife's sovereignty is retained through her son as animus personified and objectified as her lover and husband, and which leaves little to say about who is master or mistress of whom in a marriage and the destiny of progeny. There is hardly malicious intent here but the necessities of a mother's first male child to serve as her sacred Messiah, a brand new evolving and awakening of the woman's inner masculinity as complement to her feminine nature. Nevertheless, the animus rising as so archaic a Soter image equally had much to do with the boy's inner reality as well.

In that sense the animus transcended any personal relationship between Jung and his mother or an actual woman and which carried over from childhood that the archaic phallus had no feminine target. Its archetypal nature was as if a singularity in itself but which does not rule out the possibility that its ghost or phantom nature was without an object reality from an extraverted standpoint except as an unconscious erotic drive and affectation. Without distinct object measure in actual experience, however, it did play an overt "Mr. Hyde" part in the mother/Son personal relationship that carried over to the son's future relationships.

There are two possibilities here for such compression of the adversary or opponent of the father: either the phallus represented the mother's projected animus on her young son or it was simply the fact that so young a dreamer was without an anima figure that could serve as target for the giant phallus. From that hardly sexual standpoint, as Jung notes in his memoir, his child preoccupation with death is directly related to the archaic phallus as mythogenically an attribute of Hades. That morbid aspect may have been precluded at the time of his more amplified No. 1 personality, insofar as when it did come forth, at the climax of his extraversion and the end of his relationship with Freud it did so as Jung's traumatic "Confrontation with the Unconscious.[7]

In either case the "other woman" as anima is without image insofar as it is in the male psychology not connected to an "other" than mother or wife and where wife serves as mother to both her husband, and children, if there are any, in a conventional marriage. It is also true, however, that a young boy may be prematurely aroused by an "other woman" such as a little girl playmate or perhaps a schoolteacher. Jung, however, does not mention such an attraction in his Memoir and it is in general inconsequential since the premature other woman could not result in an actual erotic circumstance for a very young child. But although the great dream phallus did not arouse anything erotic for the boy, it did instead reveal itself from its complementary shadow side as its Hadean aspect and having to do with an underground cave as the subject of death, because it "probably represented a grave:" and in turn with death and the underworld as represented for him by Jesus: "At all events, the phallus of this dream seems to be a subterranean god 'not to be named,' and such it remained throughout my youth, reappearing whenever anyone spoke too emphatically about Lord Jesus. Lord Jesus never became quite real for me, never quite acceptable, never quite lovable, for again and again I would think of his underground counterpart, a frightful revelation which had been accorded me without my seeking it...Lord Jesus seemed to in some ways a god of death, helpful it is true, in that he scared away the terrors of the night, but himself uncanny, a crucified and bloody corpse. Secretly, his love and kindness, which I always heard praised, appeared doubtful to me, chiefly because the people who talked most about 'dear Lord Jesus' wore black frock coats and shiny black boots which reminded me of burials."[8] He could not justify the function of the Devil (as few of us can!) because Soter and Diabolus were fused and undifferentiated as himself, his mother's little devil dreaming big dreams of an outlandish and of a monstrous fossil phallus whose archaic magnitude had absorbed the power of The One as both God and the personal father and where the little boy son was not yet able to assume the role of Adversary to both his father and his brother.

He was, of course, without knowing in his child innocence describing the traditional notation of Evil as anti-Christ and the Devil himself except for the addition of ambivalence as represented by a phallus which in turn was the complement of Death, or the Lord of Death as Hades with his rapine appetite for the virgin Persephone, daughter of Demeter. In either case, for the child's perception and its archetypal resonance Death, as the Lord Hades, emerges in phallic form or which brotherly bonds Eros and Thanatos as a complexio oppositortum.

Apparently, as Jung matured he left Death and the Devil behind with his occluded No.2 personality that was soon enough himself phallicized as a prolific lover. The Devil, as such, was no longer associated with either Lord Jesus or the phallus and sexuality or, Death and the anti-Christ, but submerged in his No.1 *uber* personality that was singularly extraverted, outgoing, object orientated, elitist and ambitious and bent on furthering his career. Notably, however, that personality was also in service to the more introverted Freud who required a spokesman if not a salesman and front man to promote psychoanalysis as a medically acceptable healing tool. This was especially the case when both men traveled to the USA where it was expected there would be some resistance to the sexual emphasis Freud had applied to his approach and where Jung, more so as a proper gentile, would make the better impression for American Academia. Serving and following Freud's perspective thus also served to further repress the early background to Jung's No.2 personality where the mythogenic aspect of his childhood impressions, such as Jesus as the Devil and the Devil as a gross phallus, were submerged and occluded in his professional endeavors with Freud. The first signs that he was attempting to reclaim such content and its meaning came when his split with Freud was occurring and Jung retreated to the utter privacy and secrecy of composing his Black and Red Books, the latter of which included his artwork. In that case, he hears the voices of the dead as if they were seeking his counsel. But were they not his lost little boy and germinal No. 2 personality as if dead and buried in the past and thus lost of the mythogenic magic they carried for personality No. 2?

All of such amounted to his undeclared retreat from Freud that was, however, preceded by a first step that involved his intimate relation to his young lady patient, Sabina Speilrein. Enter, then, an other voice that Jung did not produce but heard, advising him to give up his role as a psychologist and take up the practice of art. That was as much saying give up your extraversion and reclaim your introversion and a lost childhood fantasy realm through the practice of art. This was the voice of his "psychotic" first patient, the young Russian Jewess, Sabina Speilrein whom he engaged in a love relationship during her course as his patient. However, who was seducing whom? Apparently, he heeded her advice to produce Art. Nevertheless, only as a closet artist was he able to come upon his Philemon whereas Sabina was seeking something more than what Freud's psychoanalytic perspective could offer. On the way for each, an intense and intimate romance transpired that was perhaps the conveying vessel of the content and meaning each sought.

The question thus remained for Jung: would there be any shortcoming if who did what or what did who was resolved confessionally as simply "I did it?" Yes and no if we take Jung at his word depending from which of his personalities it was issued. If it was from his proto-Freud extraverted personality he may have maintained interest for what reads as a mystery novel featuring Sherlock and Watson whodunits where clues are more symptoms for a criminal figure denying sexual expression and thus perpetrating neurosis, notwithstanding Detective Holmes heroin syringe. But even there and if especially so, chickens came home to roost for which personality solved "mysteries" providing there is enjoyed mainlining, or a Freudian nose for snorting up symptom clues. In either case avoiding such an extraverted approach to mysteries for the real inner object and where the detective himself is the mystery, might leave the extraverted, personality as No. 1, Carl Gustav, more content to removing the panties of virginally neurotic young ladies than the veil concealing his own inner life.

That was precisely to be the case when his mystic fantasies produced the figure of Salome, the mother of all seduction. Accordingly, forward but blind, she was but first to shed the chaff from the germ and leave Sigmund and Sherlock to their pastimes in narcosis and forced swooning into the mysteries of the infinite night. With Jung, his extraverted "mystery" and "whodunit," went soon enough beyond a question of *cherche la femme* and which was also the case for a fictionally serious Sam Spade, or what all Private Eyes and Actor Humpfry Bogart demonstrate, i.e., the detective work comes before, if at all, the feminine protagonist such as was the case in Bogart's film mystery of *The Maltese Falcon* where the craven mystery bird is the downfall of the lady involved, or disinvolved, as the apple of the detective's eye. She, as anima takes the rap and duly suppressed by the narcissistic "Private Eye." Indeed, only may the No. 1 man with great fortitude, sooner or later, risk a life digression into the nature of a Mystery older than and more often shunned by men the more preoccupied they may have been with mind over Mater, Mutter and the matter at hand, and with no distraction on the way for empathic feelings but the sniffing of M'lady's knickers. But Jung was hardly a detective and so it was otherwise with regard to the ladies who helped him bridge the stupendous content of his No. 2 personality seething to rise from his other world as a rude and monstrous phallus from the grave and realm of the dead.

Indeed, what hero but Herackles (Hercules) would join, disguised in drag, the Mystery club of Queen Omphala of Ephesus and her attendant Ladies. All ere *mystae* and initiates in the cult of revelation and for him to gain the secret of immortality by way of overcoming Death by secret aim to kill Death, The Lord Hades, and purloin his Queen of Oblivion, Lethe, the unus mundus pleroma, or simply say the *topos* of "Death." Then best to put aside the opium of pipe dreams, dress in drag and enter fully conscious for what to expect concerning the mythogenic relation of Mothers and Virgin Daughters in their traffic with the Devil or Satan: or however Mr. Death is joined below the belt with his bird in hand ready to savor a virgin mystae. Herackles would have prefered this for himself except he could not beat the Devil.

Mr. Death Personified

It is here that Jung wanders in without guile and which only his No. 2 personality is equipped to engage, altthoughbeit with one foot in Heaven and the other in the uterine passage to Hades. Mr Death does not diddle with any old virgin but the daughter of Mother Earth herself, the "Ge" lady as Mother Demeter. With her virgin daughter, Persephone. Both are in common with the Ladies of the feminine mystery epic from which most of Western religion and culture are drawn and, as such, alive and well to this day if only in the misdirected travail of neurotic and psychotic wet dreams. In that case the focus would be on Mr Death and the Other as the inner world that preoccupied Jung and his Philemon and where special notice must be taken that Death appears in figure as a phallus that, like the eternal fire of Herakleitos, forever goes out and rises up again and never subject to erectile dysfunction. This is not, of course, of my invention but offered by Jung as a dream he had of a turgidly brazen underground Devil when he was three years old.

In that case I believe Jung was merely the messenger dreaming either his mother's dream or her animus psychism common to all women in an age of animus rising, something that commenced in force by the beginning of the 19trh Century in the West and appearing full blown by the 20th. Jung is thus pre-conditioned by such gynodromia and its chthonian phallus that in classical terms is known as Hades, the Lord of Death, a figure that evolved as the Judaeo Christian Satan or, more locally in vernacular, The Devil, and which Jung indicates in the "*Christian underworld is the most celebrated snake of all, the Devil, 'that old serpent.' Actually it is a duplex pair that inhabits Hell, namely Death and the devil being characterized by the snake and death by worms.*" [9] [My italics] and both of which are phallically resembled. Hence, Hell, Hades, phallus (qua snake) and Death are rendered consubstantive and which must be kept in common when assigned in company with the bride to be virgin Persephone and then Goethean Mephistopheles.

The Devil and Death as thus terms better linking Jung and Faust with what is, non the less, originally provided by Goethe, Jung's alleged Germanic ancestor. Yet, better to leave German mentalist goose-steppers aside for Jung's nitty-gritty of *Alexandria, the city where the East toucheth the West,* and where "*the dead filled the place murmuring and said: Tell us of gods and devils,*" a subject that better accommodates a little more than Philemon who "*...had a lame foot, but was a winged spirit,*" [10] as if Oedipus (also lame foot) transcended "father murder." Jung was beginning to realize he must transcend "murdering" Freud, especially Freud kept reminding him about such "death wish" projections and which Jung so forcefully denied until it appeared in a dream. The archaic nature of the dream followed psychoanalytic expectation and with no suggestion that "murder" simply intended a separation from Freud the better Jung pursue his own budding understanding of the psyche. The "father murder" did come to pass in one of Jung's prognostic dreams. The End (of Freud) was declared by Jung in a dream he reports in his Memories Book, (December 18, 1913):

I had the following dream. I was with an unknown, brown-skinned man, a savage, in a lonely, rocky landscape. It was before dawn; the eastern sky was already bright and the stars fading. Then I heard Siegfried's horn sounding over the mountains and I knew that we had to kill him. We were armed with rifles and lay in wait for him on a narrow path over the rocks. Then Siegfried appeared high upon the crest of the mountain in the first ray of the rising sun. On a chariot made of the bones of the dead he drove at furious speed down the precipitous slope. When he turned a corner, we shot at him, and he plunged down, struck dead."

Thus, were the stars fading in Jung's eyes for Papa Freud (Sigmund qua Siegfried) set in a new dawn of the rising sun and Jung's subsequent future. The intense transference he had to Freud, so much so that he appeared in the measure of the German hero, was broken. He was, nevertheless, filled "...with disgust and remorse for having destroyed something so great and beautiful. I turned to flee, impelled by the fear that the murder might be discovered;" a murder accomplished with the aid of his inferior man untermensch (as shadow).

"I had escaped the danger of discovery; life could go on, but an unbearable feeling of guilt remained." This is more significant because Freud constantly reminded his "son" that he had a strong death wish for him and which Jung, in all his unconditional loyalty to this patriarch, strenuously denied, just as he evaded the meaning of the dream in its Oedipal context and rationalized it as having to do with "Germans," qua Siegfried, as himself who "want to achieve, heroically to impose their will, have their own way." Previously he admitted he "was unable to understand" the dream. Then the "death wish" was turned in on himself through the transference, as if he were himself Papa Siegfried qua Freud. "If you do not understand this dream you must shoot yourself" a voice reminded. "In the draw of my night table lay a loaded revolver, and I became frightened." Then he satisfied himself to blame it all on heroic "Germans" and their will to power.

Somehow Siegfried did not translate as Sigmund for him who in the German myth was the already dead brother of Siegfried, prognosticating as such the alleged (by Freud) unconscious "death wish" for himself harbored by Jung. Accordingly, this critical time of his "confrontation with the unconscious" was for Jung in fact a recapitulation of not only his childhood encounter with the devil as a monstrous underground erected phallus but the key Mystery mythologem of Western culture. His childhood notion of the Devil as Jesus and representing Death brought to bear the strong sense of guilt for displacing the father and then to absolve his sin, kill himself. Unfortunately this aspect in the story of Jesus is, and for good reason, neglected. The idea that Jesus promoted himself as the "Son of God" (the Father) was enough to determine he find his way to sacrifice on the Cross, however it would appear the Jews and Pontius Pilate were the instruments to such sacrifice. Apparently Jesus had no misgivings about this but knew he must, with himself and the Father as One, end his life. Through the Resurrection, he would forever be joined as One with the Father and the Spiritus Sancta. This was something that Jung did not appear to understand: that the murder of Freud bonded them forever as One. But this was already prognosticated in Jung's fantasy where the dead had voice and was asking him "Why?" "Why did you kill or forsake me." Papa Freud did not know why or he would have never found resolution by having the father castrate the son. Nether did Jung know why the voices of the dead father ancestors were asking him "do you know why you killed me when in fact you really wanted to be joined to me (as the Dead) forever and for all eternity and which would be the unus mundus as empty womb of the mother or a virgin filled with God as Being. But of course, from Jung's (and Plato's) hyperousia standpoint the unus mundus as First Day of Creation is the ur-pleroma of non-being filled with no more than the immanence of The Dead but not the actual dead. Why not then, the dead complain in loud voice from whoever has ear to listen or chosen by the dead to hear?

As (more) coincidence would have it, while recently editing this work I saw for the first time a French made movie called *Ja Accuse,* first filmed during 1918 after the end of WWI. The film sent me into a spin because at the moment I was heavy into Jung's Voices of the Dead, something he composed two years before (1913-1916) and during the Great War. In *Ja Accuse,* dead veterans appear to speak to a civilian population more or less not directly exposed to killing and being killed. "I accuse" for these dead soldiers and in fact asking why, to the living, did we have to die? "Did our death serve any purpose" for the living or would they go on as if nothing had happened? On the other hand, ja accuse was self-directed by the dead as if to say why did we submit ourselves to Death?

The voices of the dead were also speaking to Jung during the War. He was after all, Swiss and spared the massive carnage of young men in their prime, subject to trench warfare where en mass "over the top" they went to be machine gunned down by the thousands in a single battle engagement. Accordingly, I found it easy but extremely troubling to stretch a line from Jung hearing the voices of the dead during the war and by Able Ganze the author, director and producer of *Ja Accuse* two years later at the end of the war.[11]

Work on the film began in 1918 and some scenes were filmed on real battlefields. Abel Gance had been drafted into the French Army's Section Cinematographique during World War I, but he was later discharged because of ill health, a piece of good fortune to which he later said he owed his life. At that point, he found himself in the same position of Jung and the civilians confronted with the voices of the dead. No doubt, he felt himself "accused" and reminded as rejoined to the living before they were dead.

Apparently, for both Jung and Ganse, who lent an ear to the dead, there was a strong identification with the idea of death and the dead that stimulated their ontological anxiety. Subsequently, in order to film the battle scenes, Gance asked to return to the front and was re-enlisted into the Section Cinematographique found himself in September 1918 filming in the battle of Saint-Mihiel alongside the United States Army. His authentic footage was edited into the final section of the film. But even then there was no respite or forgiveness by the dead because "The sequence of the 'return of the dead' at the end of the film was shot in the south of France, using 2000 soldiers who had come back on leave." Gance further recalled: "The conditions in which we filmed were profoundly moving. These men had come straight from the Front - from Verdun - and they were due back eight days later. They played the dead knowing that in all probability they would be dead they before long. Within a few weeks of their return, eighty per cent had been killed."[12] Morbid as it is, in this case the binarius personality was in effect and in possession of the persona, or social mask of the personality, and the unresolved shadow or unconscious aspects of the personality and thus resulting in an identification with the underworld or Hadean realm of death. The net effect of the duplexity was the unresolvable problem of mortality and its demand for immortality, something far easier to accommodate when "feeling is all" and the knowing of thinking is at a minimum. Because in the Greek and then Christian mythos, The Dead are in the charge of Satan, The devil or Hades, Lord of Death, a literal "dead end" or finality is posited. The voices of the dead is thus that of the Adversary, mocking and taunting the living if not *Ja Accuse* means "join us" in suicide. Following that unpleasant though it suddenly brought to mind how much I enjoyed watching movies made during '30s and early '40s when I was a boy and the movies were first run. Now, some seventy years later the movie performers of the time were dead and gone except still very much alive on the screen. Indeed, now I was watching ghosts and my sense for nostalgia was dampened. The dead were speaking to me reminding they occupied my dead past and that I was enjoying living in that past as if my own death was already accomplished. The ghost screen images were now in fact speaking of closure of potential and the future. The antithesis of such finality would be the virgin nature with its immanence of potential.

"For my part, notes Jung, "I prefer the precious gift of doubt, for the reason that it does not violate the virginity of things beyond our ken."[13] Or, in other words, an advisory to not overstate what you do not know and understand. On the other hand "doubt" as the antithesis of potential presented the anomaly of a Virgin Mother, an image very much a part of the Greek Feminine Mystery religion and thereafter the Christian idea of a virgin birth.

Persephone, as the living virginity of Demeter, was certainly beyond my ken and demanded further exploration as the anomaly of a two in one virgin mother whose duplexity provided the primordial feminine nature as beginning in twoness as if in opposition to and adversary of, the divine progenitor as The One, in this case Papa Zeus, her Sire. The fact is, however, The One was not directly involved in genesis or creation of any knd and assigned this role to his No. 2 son as fallen Angel, Hades the phallic Lord of Death and Creation otherwise known in Gnosticism as Ialdabaoth and cast in the role of demiurgous. This was, however a stupendous assignment because the mother goddess more anciently in effect as Ge-meter, after Ge, Mother Earth and a mother of gods. Ge and Gai mean the earth (as in ge-o-graphy). But the Ge or De-meter mother earth included in her dominion only the topos surface of the earth where the flowers grow. This would limit the Ge-mother to the upper world of light ruled by her husband, Zeus, the brightness of day, and who is in close association with Helios, the solar deity. The realm of night, sleep and Death, on the other hand, as her womb, is interior to the earth (Chthonios), or of the infinite night underworld (Hades). The shades or ghosts of the dead populate it. The Queen of Death is Persephone, daughter of Demeter who during the winter served as consort to Hades, the Lord of Death. Accordingly, the womb of Mother Earth is her complement as the unus mundus, the transcendent world of unknowing and nothing but its pure potential, without previous impress virgin nature. Short of that Death (Hades) and the phallic snake are more directly addressed in the Thracian Mysteries of Demeter and her Virgin daughter, Persephone, who reaches her role climax as the Queen of Death and consort to the Lord of Death, Hades. Since The Lord of Death is not The One, however, his agent of genesis is doubled as Two and thus phallically predisposed. He is determined to abduct the innocent virgin, bring her below where he is the sovereign of death and the underworld and make her his Queen. The mother, in any case, had little jurisdiction in her interior or underworld daughter's chthonian venue. It is exclusively the dominion of Persephone who has suffered the strife of abduction and the violence of rape, as it were, the death of her pure and unblemished pure potential state of virginity. It is here that Hades and Hermes are combined as the subsequent purloiners of the daughter's virginity. It was the task of Hermes to bring the dead down to Hades and he was no doubt a party to the Lord of death who sought a bride. The myth, however, does not indicate that the virgin Persephone would have to be dead before she entered the realm of the dead if only it is left unmentioned that the "killing" of her virginity by the phallic Hades amounted to the same thing.

Hades and Hermes both shared not only in the business of Death but phallic personification. The duplex image of death qua phallus reminded implicitly of the phallus in Jung's first remembered dream of an underground icthyphallus, and its underworld abode where Persephone served part time as Queen and consort of Death (Hades). Appropriately, in her death role, she is known to have birthed Dionysius, the twice born god. He was thus known as the god of dismemberment in the Bacchante ritual. Stressed was the event of violent death in a succession of rebirths. In this sense, through his mother as Persephone, he was also identified with the phallic Hades, the Lord of death, as his father where he serves as the below the belt complement to the Olympian Zeus. Zeus as Father thus comes in two parts as the Heavenly Father and his lower phallic half, Zeus katacthonios, enabling him in incestuous relation with his daughter Persephone is then redefined as the Queen of Death, consort of Hades who represents the underworld phallus of death that not so curiously Jung allegedly dreamed about as a three year old child. Accordingly, his necessity for daughter incest was achieved not by abusing his own actual daughters but their substitutes as his young mistress patients, Sabina Speilrein and then Antonina (Toni) Wolff. My own interest intensifies here because Toni Wolff happened to be the analyst of my analyst who chose Toni as her analyst and avoided the choice of Emma Jung, Jung's wife who was also a practicing analyst in Zurich..

Emma as proto Mother Demeter, however, never goes below to the death-realm, but performs her *heuresus*, the ritual of search for the lost virgin(-inity) by a procession of women holding torches on their way to the sea. This commences the search for the virgin daughter, if not the original estate of virginity since lost by the mothers, after she is abducted by phallically endowed Death, keeping in mind that marriage was often ritualized by the "stealing" of the maiden by a "best man" as a service to the groom. This service would also include taking (or "killing") the maiden's virginity so that "Best Man" and raptor would be a substitute for Hades, the actual Lord of death. I would here suggest Hermes performed as best man and charged with the dirty work of deflowering the bride. Just as The One as Father in heaven requires a demiourgos to commence genesis and creation, and thus not "dirty his hands." So too it is with the in the second (binarius) place, "best man" who eventually is assigned the role of The Devil. Faust, as such, was determined to play this role and with inflated desire to play as best man for Helen of Troy. Since Faust was an extension of Goethe and Jung at one time in his life was an extension of Faust, the warning may be posted, "Virgins beware."

The Virgin Daughter thus comes to represent the lost and to be refound virginity of the mother that was stolen and in effect "killed" in the underworld of Death by its animus personification, the lustful raptor Hades. Both mother and daughter thus share this primal phallic animus not only as representing the phallic reality of the animus but that of Thanatos as well. Both images are comparable to the rising up phallus in an Underwood cave dreamed by baby Jung, They both doubled, however, as the projected animus of his mother who found herself limited to her maternal function. Accordingly, the father of the daughter and the husband of the mother receive the projection as phallus qua thanatos by which sexuality and death serve as complements one to the other. It is thus indicated that if the woman is not constantly in death and Hell, she is auto-erotically constantly fornicating as relief to dying a death that never comes. Sexuality qua death is then posed as the avenue of freedom and the awakening of the animus and its necessity to rise up in the feminine psychology. It was the position Jung's mother and then his wife Emma found themselves in at the climax of Jung's No. 1 personality anticipating as such his fall as ostensibly the binarian angel during his confrontation with the unconscious and psychotic episode. He is indeed about to become the "Red One," the Devil himself, perhaps early on prognosticated in his Red Book where he wrote: "I know just as little who you are, as you know who I am. Surely this Red One was the devil, but my devil. I earnestly confronted my devil and behaved with him as with a real person. This I have learned in the Mysterium to take seriously every unknown wanderer who personally inhabits the inner world, since they are real because they are effectual."

His Devil indeed as if he could lay claim to an archetype, personalise it, or better say identify with it as he egolessly trips the light fantastic in Hell. His only criteria for filial relationship with the Devil was he took him as a "real person," and which is a risky reason, taken seriously or not, to identify with "every unknown wanderer who personally inhabits the inner world." Either Jung with this attitude was a very brave man or a jackass, or he had not fathomed yet that his role in redness as the Devil would be to marry the Queen of Death. This, however is Jung as personality No. 2 where such comporting with the shadow world is par for the course. For Jung No.1 alarm bells would have gone off for the good Doctor, warning against identifying with an ur-bild. No. 1 would certainly not entertain any desire to have the Queen of Death as his consort or indulging in an erotic fantasy with regard to the duplex image of a Virgin Mother.

Since Mother and Daughter, as the Demeter/Kore of the Mystery religion is, in fact, one person in two parts, it is the maiden daughter aspect of Demeter that plays the active role in the Feminine Mystery religion. It was focused on the events in the underworld endured by the initiates (mystae). Her title as Queen of Death indicates death as the required state for the commencement of the mystery process of birth and transformation of the Virgin nature. "Death" in effect also amounts to her loss of virginity. Her sire, Hades, is not only the Lord of Death but equally known for his rapine proclivities and phallic demonstrations as would be the case for all good Daddies with their inscrutably secret incest wish..

Such archaic sexuality indicated the mystery process of rape, death, transformation and rebirth, All involve something primordial, a *radix sancta* invested in the state and being as the *ur-bild* of Death and, ontologically substantiated as the image of Death as Hades. His underworld denotes an unseen, or invisible place or space, as would be the case with Death: as place or house of the dead. The older form of his name was *Ais*, which means house, and then *Aides,* or *Aidonaeus,* literally Papa as Lord of the house and family. All signify the invisible interior, literally, a contained place or space or, more to the point, a womb to both creation and death that in itself is the pleroma of "nothing," and as such what is Biblically identified as the First Day of Creation, or that first day before the Binarius angel fell to commence the Second Day of Creation.

Notably, however, *house, place, space* or *topos* of the invisible (the dead) would not be in complementary opposition to a virgin state as "without previous impress" and what Plato referred to as "Chora" (*xwpa)* or space as receptacle) in his Timaeus. A non-invaginated space was equally favored in the male preference for a virgin and as if it were of a particular extra-sexual necessity for fulfilling his own dormant potential, something not provided in his mother or wife. The virgin state and potential are consubstantial and thus factor as the prima materia for a coming into being except to be reminded by Aristotle that its ousia, or essence is as void and empty and only in that condition qualified as the apieron of unconditional potential. The Aristotelian potentia as such takes on material form but as proto-hyle or material physis as without previous impress, or virgin.

The Lord of Death as animus supreme must, accordingly, choose Persephone *parthenos* as his consort in the house of death. The virgin nature, as such, indicates the entelechal nature of potential. In addition, of course, the potential for the phallic Hades would be death as the prerequisite for what's new and coming into, being. It was considered, nonetheless, from the feminine standpoint that invasion of a virgin womb was synonymous with Death, as it were, the death and abortion of potential, in this case, as purloined by an animus figure of devilish proportion, a seducer more raptor than lover, more adversary than agent of empathy. The philandering husband, as such, takes on image as this particular animus in his extra marital relationship with a young woman who has little resemblance to either mother or wife but: the mistress as a phantom or ghost anima, *La creatura* as psychoid or as if both psychic and in the flesh, actual.

It is also, however, the unconscious yearning of mother and wife to re-experience the death of virginity and its state of potential realized as birth and motherhood just as in cyclic return the psychological death of the mother is a reversion to her virgin rights of origin. In this sense the mother\ wife figure is charged with Psychologically searching for the philandering husband's young mistress and in thus identifying with her virtually reclaim their own girlish nature as daughter or little sister. Notably, as mother and wife the woman has lost status as an anima seductress capable of seducing the male. The role of anima is thus as the inscrutable *femme fatal* that is, as such irresistible for the male in his mid-life crisis. Making love with Mss Death is, of course, the via regia to the unconscious and with no less a woman who is a Queen. However, would the philanderer know he is literally in for Hell and that the mistress has already submitted herself as the archetypal bride of death. Jung indicates as much by reporting his "confrontation with the unconscious" and when he was courting psychosis.

In either case, Death qua phallic animus image is also the vital agency of transformation. What does, however, come into being through the unconscious activity of the animus is the husband. He becomes the extra marital lover and assumes the Hadean animus role. Subsequently there are two major effects as the peculiar bond of the wife with the mistress and the arduous necessity of the husband to service both in his duplex nature as Papa Zeus on high and his underworld complementary nature as Zeus katacthonios. Such was the case for Jung who served as the animus for his first patient, a young Russian Jewess. Little did he realize that he had Salome, the archetypal seductress on his hands who was a shade less than Persephone, the queen of death, and who would accordingly view his invaginating organ as the instrument of death and dying, something momentarily experienced during orgasm but in her case as indicated in her diary as a fantasy of birthing Jung's child aptly called Siegfried. In that case, the wife assumed the role of mother and with the mistress as her invisible because virtual daughter, joined as such as the single image of virgin mother. The relation is induced because of the husband's sexual traffic with both Emma and Sabina and which follows the rule of the Olympian Papa Zeus on high mating with his wife Demeter and through his below the belt counterpart, Zeus Katachthonios, the underworld Zeus as phallus, doing his own daughter. The relationship, however, is presage to the death, or descent into the underworld of the wife and her own transformation. If she does not choose such a descent she remains in the purgatory of a humdrum and meaningless life and suffered as the bitter, rejected and cast off woman.

The Divine Weakness of Thinking

Jung's *ur-reality* concept of a maternal unconscious also transcended a more parochial psychoanalytic approach along with the entire organon of philosophy from Anaximander to Heidegger where Mater qua Matter is only subliminally combined in any intensive concern for the nature of Matter. Matter, after all, was the major concern of the pre-Socratic physikoi in its considered sense as proto-hyle (original matter). Better, say psychologically as Mater or Mother. The *archai* (original) primacy of the maternal estate, however, remained to this day as *lethe*, the concealed. Indeed, Jung's consideration of a maternal unconscious had an ancient foundation but only as extracted, from lethe and the unmentionable Mater banned to thinking. In that respect materia, from the psychogenic standpoint, performed as the mother substrate to collective psychological phenomena if not the lethe tradition of philosophy from the pre-Socratic to Nietzsche and now Heidegger. Such genderizing of culture and the work of the spirit was already in evidence in Freud's super imposition of a uterine analog to focus the nature of psychology and its pathological affectations as hysteria. In either case, a concept of the collective re-direction was subtexturally predicated as maternal and as the *ur-grund* for the evolving culture by its pioneer Psychological innovators.

As much happens more overtly in modern philosophy for a student of Heidegger. The post-Hedeggerian *pensiero debole* (weak thinking) called for by Gianni Vattimo represents the feminine resistance to the animus and its masculinistic pretense to "strong thinking.". It is better defined as a philosophical thinker's identification with the feminine. *Pensiero debole* that would better serve the transgendered male "Thinker," to which Vattimo openly subscribes, as well as to a woman ruled by her animus. "Weak thinking," as a philosopher's mode would, accordingly, stand itself against the philosophical tradition from Aristotle to Heidegger and ruled by the "strong thinking" of men. In either case, such strong thinkers would stand out as animus personifications from the standpoint of the feminine psyche. Certainly Vattimo, who is a pre-psychological thinker, does not indicate the feminine as the agency of *pensiero debole* and for which he would be considered an unwitting promoter of animus rising. On the contrary, in his dialectical Marxian reasoning, weak thinking easily inverts to feeling, the typological opposite to thinking that for Goethe's Faust indicated *gefhul ist alles* as reserved for women. Thus, the old pre-Jung formula carries forth for Vattimo: "thinking" for men and "feeling" for women.[14] More alarming in such a view is the inferred weakness of the feminine nature and which is favored as the better alternative to "strong" heterosexual masculinity. Since Vattimo is both openly Gay and a Marxist, his option for matricentricity simultaneously individual and collective, indicates the new age of the male in the gynotropism at hand known as the "Nanny" or proto Marxoid State."

Where, however, and how was the male nature involved in Freud's uterine psychology and Jung's materialization of the Spirit remained obscure until the correspondence of Spirit and the animus was realized. In the collective tradition of culture, the feminine and the woman herself remained no more than an object presence in the collective expression of the animus. Hence, a correspondence by which psyche and collective tradition are not directly related. One is neither the cause nor the epiphenomenon of the other. The simultaneity also involved a relativity of male and female persona affectation and all of which included an ontological concern for the potential of coming into being of not simply for the collective culture at hand but the individual and its gender identity. The current psychological problem here was that the individual was directly related to the psyche whereas the Spirit, now as the animus at large, no longer serves except as the collective culture forms retained by Religion, Western theological systems, d the philosophical tradition and more recently as the plethora of ideologies maintained as a form of political narcissism. The animus is apparently treading in areas of political action such as the various Socialisms of the 20th Century and their matricentric priorities of ruling whole societies reduced to a kindergarten collective mentality where the ur-mutter knows best through the voice of her atrophied son as Great Dictator. Its latest global constituency would be the abbreviated voices of the faceless dead seeking presence in the cybernetic unus mundus of Twitter and Facebook.

Transgenderized Culture

Today's unfashionable "what is that thing between my legs for," is hardly a question held in the rhetoric of Transgenderized culture. It was already in evidence in Freud's super imposition of a uterine analog to focus the nature of psychology and such pathological affectations as hysteria. The term insofar as it pertains to women was derived from the ancient notion that a woman's problems were eventuated when her uterus migrated through her body and where it located itself became the seat of her malady. In either case, a concept of the collective re-direction was subtexturally predicated as maternal and as the ur-grund for the evolving culture by its pioneer Philosophical and Psychological thinkers. As much happens more overtly in modern philosophy for a student of Hegel. The post-Hegelian *pensiero debole-* (weak thinking) called for by Gianni Vattimo represents the feminine mode of "thinking." It is equally defined as a philosophical thinker's identification with the feminine. *Pensiero debole* and would thus serve the transgendered male "Thinker," to which Vattimo openly subscribes, as well as to a woman ruled by her animus or subliminal "maleness." "Weak thinking," as a philosopher's prerogative would, accordingly, stand itself against the philosophical tradition from Aristotle to Hegel and Marx as ruled by the "strong thinking" of men. In either case, such strong thinkers would stand out as spiritualized personifications from the standpoint of the feminine psyche and its *pensiero debole*. Certainly Vattimo, who is a pre-psychological thinker, does not indicate the feminine as the agency of weak thinking and for which he would be considered an unwitting promoter of animus rising and the coming into a popular cult of feminism made up as a cadre of *men without penises,* i.e., the animus woman, hoping to shed feminine "weak thinking." On the other hand, in his dialectical Marxian reasoning, weak thinking easily inverts to feeling, the typological opposite to thinking that for Goethe's Faust indicated *gefuhl is alles* (feeling is everything) and reserved for women and their power of weak thinking that is something other than the negation of strong thinking. Thus, the old pre-Jung formula carries forth for Vattimo: thinking for men and feeling for women. More alarming in such a view is the inferred weakness of the feminine nature and which is favored as the better alternative to "strong" heterosexual masculinity. Simultaneously the individual and collective indicating, as such, the new age of the male in the gynotropistic society at hand, indicated for example, by the current American Commander in Chief, as a persona (Masked) affectation of a weak thinking and passive President who is in fact without transparency yet silently at work with a secret political agenda. This was precisely the sneaky (weak thinking) trespass of Vattimo when he produces a book aptly called "Nihilism & Emancipation" by which meaninglessness predicates freedom. This goes far beyond the "double think" of George Orwell and in the post modern world prevails as the "double cross" of emancipation and by which freedom and liberty are no longer consubstantive. Maleness is then reduced to a "Metro Sex" what in the past was known as a Fop, Dandy or in the early American case, as a male who stuck a feather in his cap and called himself a "Macaroni,' an appellation that would please the Italian Vattimo. Cromwell, who butchered the Irish was also a Metrosexual personality, fastidious in dress, fragrant perfumes, body oils and soaps made from Olive Oil rather than stinking fish or meat oils and lard. The term "Metro" indicated the Fops preference for urban centers where shops offering such delicacies were abundant...

This would indicate "maleness" reconditioned by the impact of political matricentricity (including traditional marxoid socialism but long a tradition in Britain with its abundance of powerful Queens set in precedence by Queen Boudicca of ancient Britain who was a nemesis for its Roman colonizers. No doubt, the Romans in Britain set the pace for the Dandy or Fop where the better posture of the male is to pretend he is a weak and hence effeminate thinker and which is effected thereby as his persona. On the other hand, the once upon a time male strong thinker is characteristically up front in his views and intentions as would be the case with Ronald Reagan with Bubba Pres. Clinton as the halfway house in-between strong and weak thinking. In the present case, (Obama) the Presidential persona must feign strong thinking to compensate an inability to strongly think the nation's way out of an economic crisis. In all cases, the persona serves as personality mask to preclude all transparency. For their general amiability and accommodating personalities both Presidents Clinton and Obama wear, if not by calculation, the metrosexual masks to earn wide public adoration. A certain amount of effeminacy is thus made the persona opaque, lest it be clear they wear their anima on their chest as a soldier wears his war ribbons and medals.

The historically classic example of this is the Machiavellian persona: "the employment of cunning and duplicity in statecraft or in general conduct" [Oxford English Dictionary]. But that has been as common throughout history as the beans on Jack's beanstalk reaching to heavenly heights of not only the new male as the strong thinker pretending to *pensiero debole* but to support itself in a soteriological role as willing martyr and sacrificant but with hardly a mind to end up on the Cross or blow himself up and be rewarded in heaven with 72 virgins. No, that is not what our *Uuomo Nuova* qua Metro is about and if an example is needed "Mr

President" is better addressed as "Mr Soter (savior), by *arch* Conservative as well as Liberal pundits who prefer the President as "The Anointed One." What is inferred here is that the strong thinker qua *pensiero debole* is in fact a *faux* or Soter, as "anti-Christ," That, of course, outdoes the typical Machiavellian persona and in effect lends a theological, or divine and holy dimension to a political circumstance and which may be accounted for as the proliferation of political narcissism. Such is the case today where a large majority of the American public is, beyond political rhyme or reason, worshipful to The Anointed One as their inspirational and imperishable leader. It would indicate the future of a political socialist matricentric form of government is about to regress to a "Theological Military Complex" as was the case with the Islamic Ottoman Empire and: the "Sublime Ottoman State" of Turkish hegemony which lasted from 1299 to 1923 and sustained by Islam's forceful policy of Jihad from its inception. Byzantine Christianity was overwhelmed and no longer a part of the Holy Roman Christian empire.

It goes without saying that military pomposity earmarked in the flamboyant military uniform is a mass demonstration of the metrosexual predisposition where men with men was the preferred venue. It was less erotic in display but revealed the metrosexual need for cosmetic appeal. Nevertheless, along with such collective vanity went deadly intent, as was the case with Cromwell.

As the largest coherent military force since the fall o Rome, by 1800 The Ottoman Turks had occupied all of Constantanople as well as Greece, Albania, Macedonia, the Balkans and to the European border of Austria-Hungary. Then something strange happened. A brand new nation entered the scene and whose mode of government was not top-heavy with State control and the European tradition of political rule. Such loose federation was unheard of and marked not only absolute independence from Great Britain but all of the political statism of the Euro tradition as it prevailed since the middle Ages. Freedom for all and "don't tread on me," and emblemed with a coiled rattlesnake ready to shrike representing the public right to bear arms and resist any proto-European mode of totalistic State control of the people. But even worse it declared freedom of religion for the people and which masked the rule that the Roman Catholic Church would no longer enjoy political and religious hegemony in partnership with the State. In the end this equally applied to the resistance to a political ideology ruling the State. The emblem of the coiled rattlesnake prepared to strike indicate the immanence by law that publicly organized armed militias were always ready to maintain the people over the state. There were a few internal skirmishes to that effect. The real test came when the new country was faced with intimidation by foreign nations to intrude on it public sovereignty. Jefferson was already worried that the American event was in fact a "Revolution" whose effect would have been one full turn around to arrive back where it started as rule by monarchy. However, the American "revolution" was by no means a revolution in its sense as a redundancy but simply a Declaration of Independence from Britain if not the entire political tradition of Europe which maintained the dark side of Roman Republicanism through its ruling emperors who had the power of Roman Legions in hand and ready to, and with very little parliamentary mandate, go into action to put down any contention of its colonies. Consequently, Caesar effected a massive slaughter of restless Gaul where thousands of men, women and children were put to the sword. Such Euro maintained "Romanism" now effected as various brands of "Socialism," whether of the utopian or dystopian kind, were the antithesis to the political ideals of Thomas Jefferson that were then expressed as the totalistic rule by the Pope or political Monarchists. With foresight in mind, Jefferson was firmly convinced that a strong Navy represented the power of Monarchy. As a result he dismantled the US Navy that was so effective in the War for Independence, perhaps neglecting, Unlike Franklin understood that the new nation was part of a family of nations. During the war he was stationed in Paris and prevailed on the French to provide John Paul Jones with fighting ships which they did and John Paul proceeded as a pirate to raid and loot English seaside villages (cf., Herman Meville's hands on critical but jocular account of this in his Epic. *Israel Potter*.). The time soon came when the new nation had to energize its coiled snake abroad when its mercantile sovereignty was threatened. Moreover, strike it did, notwithstanding the pacific mood of Pres. Jefferson, in it first extra-territorial battle against an enemy that prevailed for 1500 years as the nemesis for both Europe and the Near East. The Yankee Doodle coiled snake struck at the mighty Ottoman Empire and in two battles on both sea and land and after Jefferson recanted and reorganized the US Navy and a very persistent US Marine Corps.

Both Europe and the Near East in their State oligarchies had little sympathy for this freakish new nation that resisted not only the fearsome Ottoman Turks but the destiny of the Roman Empire that never fell but merely re-divided Europe and continued on with overbearing Monarchist, Papist and in few hundred years easily slipped back into mode as "Socialist" with its totalitarian marxoid "The Head rules the Body," the "State rules the People" oligarchic ideal. Substantially, the party of nations was taken by surprise when the coiled snake, like the boy David confronted the mighty Philistine, Goliath and struck when Tripoli, a satrap of Ottoman Turkey, attacked American shipping. The fledgling little boy of a nation responded with its renewed US Navy and Marines and in 1800 and then again in 1805 each time defeated Tripoli...

Such newcomer's success was not only wondrous but also insulting to the powers that be if not more of an embarrassment for Great Britain, France, and Russia. Therefore, they encouraged The Greeks to free themselves from Ottoman rule. Now the tables were turned for Ottoman hegemony that began with the dethroning of Christianity in Constantanople. Britain was perhaps the most surprised and in its unbelief of such fledgling assertion was determined to test the New Nation and its Merchant Marine by stopping American flag vessels, board them and impressing its civilian Merchant marine crews for duty in the Royal Navy. It had no doubt in mind to regain its colony and, accordingly, landed an armed force in the in the new nations capital and burned it to the ground. Again, the "don't tread on me" snake struck.

The Ottoman Empire was finally disbanded in 1923 after it had Joined the Kaiser and was defeated by the Allies. With its vast military force gone it had to resort to covert terrorism as its means of Jihad. The question thus rests in such an example of a theological military complex ruling the known world longer than any other empire in post-Roman History. The anticipated End, therefore, is not by fire but overwhelmed by Acquarius and a global flood of One Way religion. Is such a destiny irrevocable if a new culture hero does not step forth to counter the Anointed One in the form of an authentic *pensiero debola* or better, Chief Executive as *La Creatura Femina* whose divine weakness will be in *gefuhl Ist Alles* ("feeling is everything"), e.g.: "*Die Gretchenfrage*' (from Faust by Johann Wolfgang von Goethe: GRETCHEN: Do you believe in God? / Faust: Fill your heart, as big as it is, from that And when you are completely blissful in the feeling, Then call it what you like/ Call it happiness! Heart! Love! God! Feeling is everything" (gefuhl ist alles)."

The Faustian put down of feminine feeling, however, is determined as such because it is equated as "weak thinking" as the power of feminine "thinking" and not only precluding "woman's intuition," but the nature of "strong thinking" or thinking per se, that is traditionally assigned as the predicate of *The Man* accounted for as a railroad track without curves, i.e., nothing but a non-commutative linear progression on a one way trip to Hell,: that is to say from The One out of touch in Heaven to the binarius demiourgos placed in charge of the Second Day of Creation.

Here we may note the Gnostic Ialdabaoth as the prototype to "The Two" as the binarius. Hans Jonas notes in his pioneer work, *The Gnostic Religion*:

"In the system of the Ophites as related by Irenaeus, he is firstborn of the lower Sophia or Prunikos and begets out of the waters a son called Iao, who in turn in the same way generates as a son, Sabaoth, and so on to seven. Thus, Ialdabaoth is immediately the father of them all and thereby of the creation. 'He boasted of what was taking place at his feet and said, I am Father and God, And there is non above me"….."I am the Lord and there is non else, there is no god beside me: to which his mother retorts, "Do not lie Ialdabaoth, there is above thee the Father of all, the First Man, and man the Son of Man."

The theme of the demiurgic conceit is frequent in Gnostic literature, including the Old Testament allusions: "For there ruled the great Archon, whose dominion extends to the firmament, who believes that he is the only God and that there is nothing above him." One step further in defamation of character goes the Apocryphon of John, where Ialdabaoth, for the sake of dominion, cheats his own angels by what he grants and what he withholds in their creation, and where his jealousy is taken to betray a knowledge rather than ignorance of a higher God.[15]

The Thinking Type

From his psychological standpoint, Jung defined thinking "as one of the four basic psychological functions, along with feeling, sensation and intuition. Thinking is that psychological function which in accordance with its own laws, brings given presentations into conceptual connection. It is an apperceptive activity [non-perceptive, ed] and, as such, must be differentiated into *active* and *passive* thought-activity. Active thinking, unlike perception which is autonomic, as an act of will, passive thinking an occurrence .The faculty of directed [active, ed] thinking, I term intellect: the faculty of passive, or undirected, thinking, I term intellectual intuition, furthermore, I describe directed thinking, or intellect as the rational function, since it arranges the representations under concepts in accordance with the presuppositions of my conscious rational norm"[16]

Obviously, "presuppositions" would be in the measure of collective thinking as essentially passive and undirected and closely related to feminine "thinking" but which in fact is the contrary to thinking, or feeling. Feeling is active or passive in its own right as a rational function. But, when it is a case of the exclusion of thinking it may be said as "feeling is everything" (*gefuhl ist alles*) as the measure of Faust's reference to Gretchen's belief in God and which in that sense is a put down of feminine "thinking" or, assigned in common vernacular as "feminine intuition" no doubt designed to counter the authority of masculine directed or active thinking.

Here, Jung would have reservations for such collective thinking as mere "occurrence" or "presentation" and must add: "thinking that is regulated by feeling, I do not regard as intuitive thinking, but as dependent upon feeling; it does not follow its own logical principle but is subordinated to the principle of feeling. In such thinking the laws of logic are only ostensibly present; in reality they are suspended in favor of the aims of feeling."[17] Jung would thus concur with Faust, the woman's belief in God is merely based in *gefuhl is alles*!

A collective "feeling is everything" would for Martin Heiddegger be "...only the concealing facade, of historical nexuses. As long as we know with insufficient clarity the proper essence of subjectivity as the modern form of selfhood, we are prey to the error thinking that the elimination of individualism and of the domination of the individual is ipso facto an overcoming of subjectivity. In distinction to the 'individualism' of nineteenth century, which protected the pluralism and the 'value' of the unique and had as its counter-essence the distinctionlessness of the herd, Nietzsche sees in the emergence of a new form of humanity, characterized by the 'typical.'"[18]

In other words, "the typical" and the "will" are here comformed to predicate the "subjectivity" as the expression of "selfhood" and work to suppress not only collective feeling but it's correlate as the feminist "feeling is everything." In that case, contra the masculine predication of selfhood and subjectivity it would be the equation of the Feminine per se with collective feeling: ergo "In a note from the year of 1888 (*wille zur Macht*) Nietzsche says: 'The feeling for and the pleasure in the nuance (---the proper modernity), in what is *not* general, goes counter to the drive that has its pleasure and power in the grasp of the typical...' Nietzsche understands by 'type' the subjectivity that, on the basis of the will to power, is installed in unconditioned domination and is hardened in the sense of the 'will.'"[19]

Directed or active thinking is thus assimilated as the Will to Power ostensibly to overcome not only the Feminine per se, but its form as collective thinking which, as the root of the matter, must perform under the nexus of *gefuhl ist alles*, and which must be overcome through the will to power. An act of violence is thus inferred insofar as the will, as the agency of power, for the achievement of "subjectivity" and its telos of selfhood implies a drive toward its type, "the *preference for questionable and frightening things.*" Here, Heidegger must defensively balk as if avoiding the subject of the will to violence by announcing: "Nietzsche is not 'preaching' here an unbridled morality or a special 'philosophy' for Germans, but instead he is thinking as the thinker he is, beings in their Being. He thinks what *is* in world history, what, because it already is, is only coming."[20]

In terms of the coming of the Third Reich, this makes of Nietzsche either its prophet or its instigator. It is, however, more in the vernacular of Heidegger's endorsement of the Parmenides tautological or self-predicating It Is (because it is), Being is because it is, soon enough becomes a political reference of "what is" in world history, "already is" as its coming. Hence beings in their Being become mutually and tautologically predisposed. The tautology, however is not a problem for Heidegger "soon as we cease to interpret Nietzsche's metaphysics according to the bourgeois ideas of the end of the nineteenth century and instead conceive it within the historical nexus to which it belongs exclusively, i.e., on the basis of its relation to the metaphysics of 'objective' idealism and to Western metaphysics as a whole, we recognize that Nietzsche's concept of the 'superman' manifests the counter-essence to the 'absolute consciousness' of Hegel's metaphysics. But we will understand neither if we have not adequately understood the essence of subjectivity" [21]

Whose particulars are gained through the will to violence, curiously enough, Hegel's 'absolute consciousness' as spiritual idealism, because couched in dialectics, is easily stood on its head to arrive as Marx's idealism of Dialectical Materialism. Would it be that the inversion of collective feeling and *pensiero debola* coincides with materialist idealism and its political expression as the new Socialist age of gynotropic collective matricentricity otherwise known as the "Nanny State." Then Vattimo was right, after all, in his conclusion that nihilism is the predicate of emancipation yet failing to note that such emancipation is the final perfection finally realized as Death!

The World: Wild and at Large

The coincidence is hardly acausal but engendered as an historical chain of events that cannot be unwound in the late evolution of Western culture except anticipated, for one example, by the American Masonic motto on the obverse side of the mighty American buck, the one dollar bill. It serves notice in *Novus Ordo Seculorum* not only as the end of historical Christianity, euphemized as The Church (meaning the Papacy) but organized religion, per se. The only measure of organization or institution (to place in being) would be The State and its totalistic order. Effected is a form of political syncretism that is little different than the syncretism of religion by Jung under the aegis of *The Psychological*, insofar as the wide use Jung makes of Religion, Religious Experience and their mythogenic radii are all compressed in the service of an *in seclorum* science of psychology. The reduction would include Buddha, Mani, Christ and Mahomet, et al, as one grand unity that must to serve its purpose as an *unus* that must blur their differential natures.

Jung began by describing a transcendent unitary God-image beyond duality as the original creative source of the unfolding manifestation composed of all manner of dualities and pairs of opposites, neglecting to point out that the unus, in its similitude to the Biblical First Day of Creation is a Void and Chaos where all differentia are no more than pre-dispositions to form insofar as the unus mundus, one world, which he defines as a Transcendent creative source beyond space and time, yet, a potential world composed of multiplicity contained in unity. What is fudged here is the difference between unity and fusion, that is, parts that are fused in identity and utterly lost of difference. That is perhaps the sum of the problem that compromised Aristotle's concept of *entelecheia*, whose philosophical premises were rendered alchemical by the Arabs and Jews of ancient Alexandria. It was, however, further disturbing that Jung had virtually ignored this old wizard's concept except to come by it second hand in his study of alchemy where he focused instead on the 16th Century German alchemist, Gerhard Dorn's fixation on the unus mundus and which made it, as did Jung, the all of process whereas for Aristotle it was more the precondition for potentia. No doubt the rich iconography of medieval alchemy hooked Jung's faculty for creative fantasy and imagination. As much might be said for the modern "comic book" as illustrated broadcast of the Superman as paradigm of the Western will to power, fame, fortune and success if only in the privy of one's own unus mundus.

PART TWO: *PAN HERMETICA*

Petrification of the *Prima Materia*

The philosophical premises of Aristotle were compromised by the Arabic and then German, post Acquinus and Paracelsus German alchemy, Both fixed on the "Stone" or Lapis as "original, or "arche matter." The Aristotelian notion *of etelecheia* was thus compromised because Aristotle's prima materia could no longer be understood in its relation to his prima materia as predicated by apieron, or boundlessness. The latter had already been "Christianized" or theologized as the unus mundus and thus limited to The One as Godhead, indicating it was no longer available for empirical demonstration and alchemical manipulation. The prima materia as "hard rock" thus displaced the transcendental (*hyperousia*) apieron as no more than prime substance or physis (nature) understood only in terms of an element without its qualia. This, however was already accomplished by Thales who mistook apieron for the element of water so that arche matter was nominalized as hylos. Followed was Anaxemenes notion that air (pneuma or aer) was the prima matter and in turn Herekleitos' fire as arche and finally for Leucipus and Democratus who reduced apieron to earth as arche and by which "atom" and arche became synononomous as matter in its smallest state. In all cases such reductions were an attempt to render apieron to sense perception when in fact it was no more than a category of the eidos and a conceptual understanding, or what later Kant classified as the noumenal thing in itself, that in itself had no visible quality. The attempt at reification of the eidos, however, was instituted as alchemy where a hands on or empirical relation was taken concerning material substances. Instrumental to this was Aristotle's process procedure that he called entelecheia as an internal process of a material substratum (hypokemimenon) that had special relevance to an alchemical procedure: "Aristotle's analysis of genesis in the Physics, apparently based on a Platonic prototype (of genesis)" notes Prof. E. Peters, "leads him to the isolation of three principles (archai) involved in all changes from one thing into another: the immanent form (eidos), the privation (steresis) of the form of the thing it is going to become, and, finally, the substratum (hypokeimenon) that persists through the change and in which the genesis takes place. Its name is dictated by its function; thus from a predicational point of view the substratum is that of which other things are predicated and which is not predicated of anything else. But the passages in the Physics are considering hypokeimenon (substratum) in the contest of material change, and so it is not merely an abstract logical concept but, together with the eidos, a genuine co-principle of being, what is, from a slightly different point of view: where matter (hyle) and, like matter, can only be known, not directly but analogically. Both the logical and ontological aspects of hypokeimenon persist in later thinkers..."[22]

Prof. Peter's thus provides not only a concise and definitive summation of the original Aristotelian intention but from the standpoint accounting for the alchemical modus operandi as it is derived in Alexandria. But, by the time of Gehard Dorn the Aristotelian proto-hyle or ousia (as pure and unconditioned potential of hypokeimenon) was virtually transubstantiated or "Christianized" as a God-like unity or Unus mundus as pleromatically resembled to "the world." This object fixed *petra* and upside down "word made Flesh" equally finds the flesh through *creatura* made Word as a decarnation of what was already reified as the Lapis or stone holding Hermes captive in its obdurate and impenetrable mass. The notion thus also later corrupts an assumed identity in the Black Stone at Mecca fallen from the heavens as Satan himself and thus kept in the courtyard, banned from the mosque. In other words, apieron was a concept banned by both Christianity and Islam but It appealed enough to Jung and his interest in Alchemy and enough to surface, accordingly, in the microcosms of his Analytical Psychology as the unus mundus or, as paraphrased by Marie-Louise von Franz: "In that potential, unity world, we are told, all the 'pious' will be united Outside time, for the unus mundus does not exist within the space-time continuum,"[23] and which is the proto-analytical and thus tautological (self-predicating) way of speaking of retro-fitting a new concept of the Hereafter for a secular (psychologized) approach to soul, psyche and their perpetuity beyond the grave. In that case, post-mortem, the soul is accommodated in the *lethe* (oblivion) of the unus mundus totally lost of its relation to apieron as a transcendental hyperousia that is then psychologically replaced by steresis and the predicate of negation as the "un" conscious. Although the concept of Resurrection is also eventuated during the Alexandrian epoch, the very term "unconscious" indicates a vacuous and empty place whose logic is derived through the logic as a via-negativa by which it is defined by what it is not. But even more ludicrously the psychoanalytic of Freud and the Analytical Psychology or Jung cannot refrain from assigning the unconscious as a "substratum" (*hypokeimenon*) filled with the memorabilia of conditioned experience as a repressed content or, in Jung's case, added to by his borrowing what amounts to Aristotle's notion of "immanent form" and potentia to predicate an endopsychic (substratum) archetype however reminiscent of the Greek eidos or Kant's noumen as ding an sic. In either case, The Analytical attempts to define a predisposition to form or the immanence of the eidos by the archetype or that which is beyond representation until allowed form as an image. Such psychologistic adaptation, however, is not faulty in aping Greek philosophy but manages to evade, accordingly, the ontological anomalies and paradoxes tendered and accommodated in Greek thought. Prof. Philip Wheelwright, in his work on Heraclitus notes, for example, "…if metaphor and paradox are to serve a metaphysical purpose, each must to some degree involve the other. If metaphor is employed without a touch of paradox, it loses its radically metaphoric quality and turns out to be virtually no more than a tabloid simile. If paradox is employed without metaphor it is no more than a witticism or sophism. The double principle is so important for understanding Heraclitus' more obscure fragments that it is worth while to look at each of the two complementary aspects separately."[24] The duplexity combining metaphor and paradox had already visited Jung in his metaphysical excursions, e.g., "Nevertheless, with regard to the down side of this urge to submerge in The One."

Jung was cautiously aware of what would occur if he succumbed to such fate proposed for him by von Franz when he notes that, whereas "The One is The fourth, Dorn saw in the quarternity the absolute opposite of the Trinity, namely the female principle, which seemed to him 'of the devil,' for which reason he called the devil the 'four-horned serpent.' This insight must have given him a glimpse into the core of the problem. In his refutation he identified woman with the devil because of the number two, which is characteristic of both. The devil, he thought, was the binarius itself, since it was created on the second day of Creation, on Monday, the day of the moon, on which God failed to express his pleasure, this being the day of 'doubt' and separation." [24] Following this von Franz observes in a footnote: "The binarius which has no middle term, is without a link, and signifies division. Nevertheless, the ternarius, which has a middle term, is the sign of concord and conjunction. For it is the first of the odd numbers, and the first wholly unequal, whence as it were all is concord.... And when the singer of Mantua [Virgil] said, God rejoices in odd numbers,' it is as if he said: God loves peace and love, for he is himself peace and love."[25] In that case, the feminine qua even numbers, fares the worst in the eye of God, notwithstanding the goddess Aletheia (Truth) that judges any usurpation of the wisdom of God (Sophia) must fall into matter and which at once indicates The Word became flesh as a fall of God's wisdom, the Logos or unspeakable Divine Word, the "matter" of a mortal being if not being itself conceived by the binarius, the Devil himself. It is further judged that this mortal being is guilty of instigating the fall or purloining from God of the Logos and might accordingly be said as the original, original sin. Obviously, the mortal being is in simultaneous identity with the Immortal God and as such, one and the same, so that it is a case of God talking to himself as He did with Job. What are indicated here is what God steals from himself by way of the mortal being, the profane anima as Sophia or Aletheia. Avoiding the metaphysical implication of the anima as mediatrix von Franz prefers to psychologise it "...when the 'pleromatic' anima --the anima as an archetype of the collective unconscious--is projected into matter with the result that, although not recognized as a psychic content, she is nevertheless brought considerably nearer to the sphere of human understanding."[26] What remains tautologically self-predicating here is that God's anima as Sophia is without an object, place or being to "fall" into insofar as the mortal being and the Immortal God are from a psychological standpoint, mutually identified. From the metaphysical standpoint, however, that is not the case insofar as God remains transcendendant and a Being other than the human in being. Subsequently what the psychological view, because secular and non-transcendent, avoids, is the distinction between Being and beings (On and Ontos) and notwithstanding Parmenides when he infers Being is because it is because Being is "Is," whereas the diminutive little being is yet to come into being when it becomes aware that the transcendent "big" Being and God are one and the same. Otherwise God remains no more than the imago dei or what Jung postulates as the purely psychological image of God. This is precisely the reductive standpoint that holds Sophia (wisdom) as no more than Creatura, or the anima as the Gnostic Sophia Prunicus (wisdom the whore) limited, as such, to the feminine as binarius and whose animus is the Devil.

Death and the *Unus Mundus*

In Jung's case both *Lethe* (oblivion) and Death was materialized as the unus mundus as final unity and no less an ontological state of a post partum Death qua Nihil, combination. The two notions were strangely overlapped except Jung had grounded the unus mundus in his idea of the prima materia derived in his study of alchemy, rather than first hand from Aristotle. Equally approached second hand from the alchemist Gehard Dorn[27] it served to confound the Aristotelian prima materia, or proto-hylic essence of matter with the unus mundus, indicating that the original concept had gone through a number of changes and interpretations ranging from the neo-Platonists to Plotinus to Thomas Acquinas. Yet, Jung is fully aware that the revised paradigms for the unus mundus are drawn from the Genesis idea of the First Day of Creation. Certainly there is a parallel between the two but which carry with it the variety of interpretations serving various philosophical and theological points of view that would condition the psychological conclusions and significance Jung would draw.

More likely the alchemical view and its tradition stemming from the Alexandrian Arabic influence would in fact invert or otherwise corrupt the Aristotelian understanding of entelechy. As much is indicated when Jung, following Dorn, notes: "For him the third and highest degree of conjunction was the union of the whole man with the unus mundus" or otherwise joined in the first day of creation when nothing was not yet in actu. Dorn's highly speculative theological, philosophical view is not, however, drawn from actual alchemical work or Opus and so he would not have been versed in the shortcomings of alchemical kitchen work. "The adept," notes Jung," had to experience again and again how unfavorable circumstances or a technical blunder or--how it seemed to him--some devilish accident hindered the completion of his work, so that he was forced to start all over again from the beginning."[28] The actual work, or what Aristotle referred to as *energeia* of the entelechal process, would be foreign to Dorn, who "understood," notes Jung, "the alchemical *solutio* primarily as a spiritual and moral phenomenon and only secondarily as a physical one." There is a contradiction here as Jung notes:

The dogma of the Assumption and the alchemical mysterium coniunctionis express the same fundamental thought even though in very different symbolism. Just as the Church insists on the literal taking up of the physical body into heaven, so the alchemists believed in the possibility, or even the actual existence, of their stone or of the philosophical gold. In both cases, belief was a substitute for the missing empirical reality.[29]

Jung's criticism again combines paradox and metaphor as a far-fetched comparison of church doctrine that the physical body goes post-mortem to heaven with the alchemical notions about the Lapis and their gold as "missing empirical reality." Jung's notions about "archetypes" and a "collective unconscious" would also be purged by such criteria. More likely he is chaffing at the bit for the lack of any empirical evidence that there is or is not much evidence for his own Hereafter. The "missing empirical reality," however, was included in Aristotle's entechal theorem as *energeia* and the work" or opus involved in the practice of alchemy. Jung's substitute for actual alchemical practice was, however, his practice of sculpting and closet work on his Redbook. In either case the empiricism involved was a "hands on" relation to the work.

Early on in Alexandria the pioneer of alchemy as an empirical opus, was Maria Prophetessa known as handy in the kitchen and innovative with her pots and pans that were soon adapted as alchemical laboratory apparatus: Although her theoretical contributions remained influential into the middle ages and beyond, Maria was more famous for her designs of laboratory apparatus. Likewise, Babylonian women chemists used recipes and equipment derived from the kitchen. Thus, ancient alchemy was identified with women, and the work of the early alchemists occasionally was referred to as *opus mulierum*, or "women's work." Consistently enough, by the time of Gehard Dorn, creatura, or the woman was identified as Binarius, the twoness of the Devil. This mother in negation of all mothers may very well represent the blank and vacuum womb as the unus mundus and in position as a first day as a virgin womb. Any thought of becoming absorbed and united with such an *unus uterus* that was barren and, as von Franz notes "does not exist within the space-time continuum." Dorn's wish to unite himself with or in such a terminally virgin womb would amount to a coniunctio as an unborning rather than the climax of mortality in death and precluding as such the possibility of Resurrection as an entelechal *ens.* Such identification of the *ens* with potentia thus bypasses energeia by which potentia is the fulfillment of the prima materia. Overlooked, as such, is the Aristotelian necessity of work, or participation through *energeia* to achieve the climax of potentia as the *dasein* of morphe or forms in appearance and the ontological presence or Being. Alternatively, it may be in reference to the ontological creation of new Life in being. Alchemically denied the ontological "new being" is trapped and captive as the Mercurious in an unyielding and obdurate Lapis or stone, but which taken from the point of view of paradox and metaphor points too the empty and void unus mundus as an unconditionally virgin womb.

Astoundingly, the Aristotelian concept of entelechaia in a compactly stated premise predates or perhaps anticipated what Jung has put forth as a process of individuation and integration of the personality by the ontological quantum called the Self that he equates with the unus mundus. He may, as such, have preceded the workless and contra-empirical position of Gehard Dorn's pro-mystica approach with no energeia (work in material reality) with the advantage of gaining forthright what Alexandrian and then European alchemy belabored for some fifteen hundred years. But, of course, I draw this conclusion in hindsight of the Alexandrian event and its five hundred year course that included not only alchemy as a precursor to modern science but the Christian event and which then climaxed as Islam. reverting to an Old Testament venue.

Premature Death: Arriving Before You Leave

Dorn's approach thus amounts to hubris or inflation by achieving death before he is born and lived and which is totally contrary to the Christian meaning. If Jung supports this he does so by contradicting himself when he cites Philo "who points clearly to the idea of the Microcosm and hence to a unity of the psychic man with the cosmos." In Dorn's case the "psychic man" is apriori dissolved or fused in the world so that the work or energeia is bypassed to affirm what is in actu as the telos or the ens. The possibility of unity is thus foreclosed because of the unborning of the psychic or pre-psychic man. Indeed, a principle of unity requires the presence of something in being and not the person as equivalent apriori with the vacuity of either the unus mundus or the first day of creation. What then results is a form of self-predication or tautology, a *circulus in probando* and which is steeped not only in a corrupted logic but psychologically the earmark of inflation in its vulgate form as "I yam who I yam, Popeye the sailor man" and with all due respect for my own time at sea as a merchant seaman.

Dorn's approach is, strangely enough, contra-alchemical process where the emphasis is on work and where the opus is the same as the Aristotelian enegeria. That would render Dorn a "Quacker" who avoids the empirical experience evoked during the alchemical opus and, as Jung well demonstrated and emphasized, evokes the psychic expression of the primordial aspects of physis or substance of matter and what Aristotle was getting at in the first place. Indeed, alchemy was a precursor to empirical and first hand knowledge of whatever phenomenon studied simply because the Opus or work and the implementation of energeia is indulged. Jung, of course, knows as much when he must conclude *"The 'unity of the soul' rests empirically on the basic psychic structure common to all souls, which, though not visible or and tangible like anatomical structure, is just as evident as it."*[30] [my italics, ed].

This reiterates Aristotle's understanding of prima materia as a primal ousia or proto-hyle that in effect is without parts or substance because it is the agency of a pure, unconditioned and unlimited potentia that through the work or as achieved through energeia becomes what it is as its ens. The two concepts certainly had much in common, except the alchemy of Gehard Dorn that Jung followed had reified and not transcended the prima materia as in fact something more than a stone (Lapis). Yet, the "work" involved was in parallel to a psychic or internal process, e.g., "... entelecheia means 'internal activity' or in some cases (where this internal activity does not remain in the subject, but which is something static, without any sense of 'doing' about it. Even in the place where Aristotle says that energeia has taken over the function of entelecheia...he is insistent that this is an extension of its primary meaning, which is that of keneosis..."[31]

Physis Contra Psyche

It is here that the alchemist departs from the Platonic view where psyche takes precedence as all movement in compare to Aristotle who simply replaced psyche with physis as nature in the material sense. Entelecheia is then either subordinate or in equivalence with energeia which combines acting on and kenesis or movement as the agency of the ens and telos as form in appearance or in being. The alchemist thus bypasses the Platonic and Parmenidian view if not the entire Hellenic approach simply because neither Alexander or Aristotle were Hellenistic Greeks but Macedonian and Thracian and even more so because from the entreme Western end of

Macedonia known as Epirote or Illyria (modern day Albania). Although there is some sympathy between Greeks and Albanians, the latter are distinct from the Pelopenesian and Mediterranean Greeks because derived from the North, if not Nordic and Teutonic warrior cultures related to prehistoric "Battle ax" cultures which not only occupied Thrace but Sparta as well. Barring the Teutonic influence in Illyria and Macedonia, Jung makes sweeping generalization by relocating European alchemy's source as, "Mandean and Sabaean remnants of Hellenistic syncretism. From them they derived a *sal sapientiae* that seemed so unlike the doctrine of the church that before long a process of mutual assimilation arose which put forth some very remarkable blossoms" [32]

Jung would therefore attribute Alexander's saying "salt is fire and dryness" as a part of Sabaean magicism when he may have just as well been referring to his countryman, Aristotle's entelecheia where potentia is the essential of prima materia. It would accordingly be placing too much on migrational and diffusionist recapitulations rather than Aristotle deriving his notions from his own immediate archetypal experience. The only conclusions to then draw would be that Alexandrian alchemy was derived or mainly influenced by a proto-Arabic Sabaean culture of a millennium prior to the establishment of Alexandria and the introduction to Egypt of the Aristotelian concept of entelecheia and where it is not only a case of reduction to material cause and proto-hylic matter but the principle of dynamis and energeia as the making *in actu* in the alchemist hope to transmute base metals in to gold or which is in effect a solarization of matter and by which it is God invested and why preceded the entelechal opus as with and for the "Immovable One," or God.. Certainly the archetypal idea of as much may have been present to Sabaean magicians but whose presence in a Macedonian Alexandria may be exclusively accounted for as no more than a culture transmigration of ideas. But this is highly unlikely insofar as it would merely reduce Alexander's idea of the sal sapientia to Sabean magicism and not from its highly developed Aristotelian source. Yet, Jung's utterance about "where the East meets the West" clearly implies each their radical difference one to the other and that the "West" or Macedonian influence was not derived in the "East" as a proto-Arabic Persian but had a separate identity that was not exactly Hellenic but included remnants of a Northern culture origin.

Indeed, that the stone had already replaced the psyche in the Arabic alchemical interpretation of Aristotle's *entelecheia*, and thus materialized it as the object of unconscious projection would have more to do with Aristotle's emphasis on physis (rather than the Platonic psyche). Jung's drawing in a sabaen influence thus stands as no more than a deus ex machina proposition. If such were the case it 500 years later missed the point of Aristotle's prima materia by later intruding the Arabic preference for the stone in its Ka'aba at Mecca, literally an unus mundus that fell from Heaven if a Jungian syncretism is enjoyed to compound Dorn with the event of Islam. Then it would be a case of the stone from the supreme Divinity as the Mother of all mothers or what satisfies Jung's definition for what he referred to as the "maternal unconscious" and then to further mix metaphors in the throes of paradox, declare Dorn's embrace of the unus mundus reduces him to an ever loving host to uniting with the maternal unconscious. Thus the climax of the Arabic development of alchemy that commenced with the appearance in Alexandria of Aristotle's work may be said to end when the stone was isolated in the courtyard at Mecca but banned in the Mosque or House of Worship. There is, of course, a connection here between the Feminine presence and its status in Islamic culture indicating it as pre-Alexandrian and related to the pre-Egyptian Sabaean culture. Be that as it may, it is an idle stretch insofar as it tends to preclude the possibility of spontaneous archetypal emergence in a culture evolution or, it may be said, an epigenetic intrusion in the collective gene pool. On the other hand, considering that the Macedonian Alexander was preoccupied as a military leader reaching his squadrons deep into the East as far as India it may also be reductively supposed that he reconditioned his mentor and master, Aristotle, with certain Eastern notions of a mystical kind. Aristotle's enlecheaia indicated that alchemy was nascent to Macedonia, however, is far from a mystical contemplation or Sabaean magicism. Jung, noted, for example, "A Greek treatise describes the alchemical process as the 'eight graves.' Alexander found the 'tomb of Hermes' when he discovered the secret of the art."[33] Or: "Alexander the Great, King of Macedonia has the following words...Blessed be God in heaven who has created this art in the salt."[34]

Salt, of course, is a reference to Aristotle's prima materia and, accordingly, with the help of God, the Immovable One. The "salt" or prima materia are thus, when prevailed as The Stone (or Lapis), marked as the void of Death and is in equivalence to what Jung called the unus mundus as noted by Gehard Dorn, That would render it in emphasis as a finality rather than the apriori potentia emphasized by the Macedonians. On the other hand, both the Book of Genesis and the Aristotelian prima materia qua potentia concur. It is however, a question of emphasis that in this case determines a point of view, i.e., whether the unus mundus & co., emphasized the primordial archai or origin ("ur") or Eschaton as death and The End. The latter represents the Christian apocalyptic conclusion and the former, the Macedonian archetypal encounter with material causality. Most significant is the fact that Gehard Dorn rejected the Aristotelian conclusion because of its involvement in matter and its proto-hylic archai. Better then to explore Dorn's view when he states."whoever wishes to learn the alchemical art, let him not learn the philosophy of Aristotle but that which teaches the truth."

Dr. Monika Wikman summarized in her book Pregnant Darkness, "Alchemists such as Gerhard Dorn, in his work 'The Speculative Philosophy,' referred to this next alchemical stage [inner healing] as Unus Mundus, where splits are healed, duality ceases, and the individual, the vir unus, unites with the world soul."[35] Dorn notes in his Theatrum Chemicum" Volume 1:

> It is the study of the Chemists to liberate that unsensual truth from its fetters in things of sense, for through it the heavenly powers are pursued with subtle understanding.... Knowledge is the sure and undoubted resolution by experiment of all opinions concerning the truth.... Experiment is manifest demonstration of the truth, and resolution the putting away of doubt. We cannot be resolved of any doubt save by experiment, and therefore is no better way to make it than on ourselves. Let us therefore verify what we have said above concerning the truth, beginning with ourselves. We have said that piety consists in knowledge of ourselves, and hence it is said that we make philosophical knowledge begin from this also. But no man can know himself unless he know what and not who he is, on whom he depends and whose he is (for by the law of truth no one belongs to himself, and to what end he was made. With this knowledge, piety begins, which is concerned with two things, namely, with the Creator and the creature that is made like unto him. For it is impossible for the creature to know himself of himself, unless he first know his Creator.... No one can better know the Creator, than the workman is known by his work.

Advisedly he notes, "truth, beginning with ourselves" but with the contingency that he first know "the Creator." Has he already assimilated the idea that the alchemical auron nostrum is the solar color and hence, an aspect of the Diety?

In view of this, the German alchemist Dorn did not derive the idea of the unus mundus from Aristotle's prima materia. The Macedonians adapted the concept from the pre-Socratic physiologoi, where Anaximander referred to it as *apieron*, or that which is without boundary or otherwise without predication in space, or *topos* and predicated in time only as exclusively eternal time rather than sequential time. This was inferred when Alexander related the salt to God, "immovable One."

Aristotle Stood On His Head

Aristotle's version was as such not imported to Europe intact during the Arabic migrations to Spain and with it the practice of Alchemy where the original Aristotelian prima materia was reconditioned as literally a stone or Lapis in the Arabic and, in turn, the European practice of Alchemy. A directed materialism thus sets the alchemical process for manipulation of physical substances losing sight, as such, of the *prima materia* as *ousia* or essence of matter. The Lapis materialism, however also resulted not only as an emphasis of Death but the feminine nature where both were the privation of a pro macho maleness and which rendered them as unconsciously archaic and hence given to repression. That would have to wait for reconsideration with the rise of Mariology, something hardly encouraged by the Church although the apotheosis of the virgin Mother was built into the theology from early on. Bypassing the corrupted alchemy, La creatura as womankind then could assume the identity of the stone would include the freed Mercurious and which, as the archaic version, would have preempted the appearance of Jesus Soter. Precluded, as such would have been the Old Testament expectation of a Messiah. Consistently enough this reverts to Alexander discovering the tomb of Hermes or it may be said the stone or rock of death harboring the Savior. Recalled here is the matricentricity of the Macedonians where Queens were in order as monarchies by the relation of Alexander to his sister Cleopatra that evolved this personification in name and repeated presence until Caesar and Mark Antony were possessed by such a *Femme fatale*. In terms of Alexandrian alchemy, on the other hand, its pioneer figure was known as Maria Prophetessa and by which the feminine nature was included in the alchemical transition as the *soro mystica*, rendered superlative to conceal the fact that the alchemist female accomplice did, as did Maria, the "kitchen work" or what went on in the alchemist's laboratory. In the Gnostic tradition that ran parallel to alchemy this feminine figure was referred to as Sophia, or Wisdom, yet predicated as Sophia *Prunicus* or Wisdom, the Whore.

Short of that, the alchemy so overwhelmed Jung that he had need to enjoy his *soror mystica* in his variety of mistresses and most intensively with his first, as Sabina Speilrein. And although not by taking his que from Alexander and his discovery of the tomb of Hermes it, as he notes, "...ultimately led to the question of Christ as a psychological figure: "As early as 1944 in Psychology and Alchemy, I had been able to demonstrate the parallelism between the Christ figure and the central concept of the alchemists, the lapis or stone."[36] Was this a psychologizing reduction of the Christ figure through alchemical Petrification, or simply a mode of displacing the meaning of Christ? If it is, then the unus mundus is inverted as the chthonion underworld, qua Death or Hell, to the effect of retaining Christ locked in the "stone" of Hell, and precluding as such His Resurrection. Part of the confusion here was because Plato's concept of psyche or soul was retranslated by Aristotle as physis but which would indicate the soul became flesh or in actu as "matter." Nevertheless, Jung notes the "Westerner...cannot see why a self should become a reality when it enters into relationship with the world of the first day of creation." And why is this but because "He has no knowledge of any world other than the empirical one."[37] But here Jung is projecting his own agnostic view on the Western collective consciousness in his need to re-invent a secular Hereafter as the unus mundus and which is as metaphysical as traditional religious views except, unappealing as the notion of Death as nothing but *Lethe* (oblivion) in the unus mundus pleroma of nihilio.

Accordingly, Aristotle's *entelecheia* is made to serve the displacement of Christ through the ultimate representation of matter as the Lapis or stone and which is understood to conceal the elixir of transformation known as the Mercurious. The alchemical opus, therefore, concerned freeing the Mercurious from its embodiment in the stone and which is an appropriate metaphor for the unavailability of the content of the maternal unconscious. In this manner Christ is regressed to the figure of Hermes (qua Mercurious) whose service is to transport the dead to Hades as was the case with the Pied Piper of Hamlin. Curiously enough, represented here is the original Germanic resistance to Christianization but which obviously enough, corresponds to the Arabic idea of freeing a geni trapped in a bottle or in a lamp as a means of being granted three wishes. "Three" also indicates Hermes Trismigustus or Hermes thrice blessed. The "wish" for Dorn was, however, for his own unity with the stone that represented the archai or ur-stone as the one and original world of the unus mundus, literally, as Jung notes it, a *mundus archetypus*.[38] Here, however, it must be observed that the archetype itself is no more than an irreprsentable immanence and, as such, at par with its receptacle, the unus mundus. In either case, the best may be done by referring to both as facultas praeformandi or no more than pre-dispositions to form.

This amounts to saying that in death qua the unus mundus such unity is achieved as a final perfection. Lost in such translation was the original idea characterizing prime or archai matter as *apieron,* or an infinite "without boundary" undefined mass as a kind of super atom preceding Creation and more recently known as the big bang and ensuing expansion of the universe. The unus mundus petrified, however, was Jung's recourse to his problematic relation to art where again Petrification remains its agency and the key to much of Jung's work: "this thing has been consistent with me, and at any time in my later life when I came against a blank wall, I painted a picture or hewed in stone. Each such experience proved to be a rite d'entree for the ideas and works that followed hard upon it. Everything that I have written this year (1957) and last year, 'The Undiscovered Self,' 'Flying Saucers: A Modern Myth,' 'A Psychological View of Conscience,' has grown out of the stone sculptures I did after my wife's death (Nov. 27, 1955). The close of her life, the end, and what it made me realize, wrenched me violently out of myself. It cost me a great deal to regain my footing and contact with stone helped me."[39]

Jung and the Stone

Stone, as such, served Jung as both his womb of creation as well as a tomb of death. In its equivalence to Death or a nihil state, Jung's affection for the unus mundus also served as the material first cause. It thus took on representation of the more ancient symbol of the ever-spinning Uroboros or tail-eating serpent and which I would cite as the primordial representation of tautology or self-predication but, in that case, as a reverse negative predication b y which the serpent devours itself and disappears, contra being, i.e., into *Lethe.*

The only active quality of *apieron,* however, was that it spun like a whirlwind or tornado from which were "winnowed out" (*apocrisis*) an active principle of opposites that stood in contention one to another. It is here that a dynamic of opposites begins as a concept and it precedes but is invested in Aristotle's understanding of the *prima materia qua potentia*. Yet, it was this concept that became the fundamental of Jung's approach to psychology and most notable when Empedocles further defined the *eide* that emerged from this prima materia as the four elements: water, air, fire and earth. Eros was thus preconceived in its uninterrupted original state as "virgin:" or in extended analog, as *apieron*, the boundless as prima materia or, if you will, the first day of creation qua the unus mundus later reified to by Arabic\European alchemy as the Lapis or stone.

It conceptually reappears more recently as a massless super atom preceding the big bang of creation. Such proto-hylic and original material states were pitted against Strife (*neikos*) and its destructive intent and where they become the causal *energeia* or "work" principl for the creation of new being in a process of palingenesis and negentropy.

The coming into being of complementary "elements" indicated not only the death of the unus mundus as in fact the death of death but the coming into being of Creation. The death of death, however, engendered a notion of a hereafter. Was this, after all, the goal for both Dorn and Jung The Christian account of Heaven, Purgatory and Hell were apparently unsatisfactory, more so the animus identification was filled out by a devilish persona well defined, at least or Jung, by Goethe's Faust. And since this newly appropriated Hereafter is towards an end, beginning and end are rendered consubstantive in a topsy-turvy ambivalence.

In the Biblical account of the first day of creation it appears as the Chaos or Void that is in equivalence to the original unus mundus as undifferentiated "first matter," *prima materia, proto-hyle*, etc., but which equally connotes in psychological terms the *ur-mutter*, "first or primordial mother" as the maternal unconscious. The goal for Jung with his unus mundus would thus be equivalent to a return, indeed, dissolution in the maternal unconscious as in fact the prima materia or archai mother. It is, of course, trite to say the unus mundus as pleroma of a hereafter, or place after death is simply a wish to return to the womb of the maternal unconscious. In either case, no matter how ell intended the re-invention of a "life" or *in being* after life it still all amounts to being in a state of Lethe or oblivion and which would be the same conclusion drawn by a confirmed atheist or agnostic.

In that case, following the Arabic rule, the ur-mutter or *matter* would be likened to a stone, a primitive notion already transcended in Aristotle's notion of *prima materia* as well as the modern notion of the relativity of time/space.

Notably, however, this prima materia must be destroyed or overcome through a process of differentiation represented by the Second Day of Creation when the Divine Demiourgos defines things after their kind. Morphe or forms in appearance would be the antithesis to the undifferentiated unus mundus. Morphe or forms in appearance are the End State of Aristotle's process of *entelecheia* that begins with pure potentia and which Jung assigned as the telos of the unus mundus. It may be noticed, however, that such a creation is equally related to Hades (as Death) and agent of destruction. It is thus inseparable from God as Creator and Being. The complementary relationship becomes more distinct between Satan and God when Hades and Satan are realized as death, the greatest evil, along with its means, destruction, and all of which falls back on the Teutonic "Twilight of the gods" or, with greater definition for *Ewige Jude* as the End of Days and the Second Coming of Christ.

Accordingly, from an ontological standpoint, the idea of God is stood synonymous with that of Being whereas non-being was indicated not as Death and destruction but the unus mundus and the first day of creation. The speculative nature of the super atom would thus enjoy an ambivalence that includes at once the expansion (creation) of the universe and its simultaneous destruction as the contraction of the universe in its paradigm as "Black Hole." Such as it is the universe prevails only in the meantime or time in-between both extremes: a notion sympathetic to biblical eschatology. In that sense non-being represented the negation of Being, suggesting that Satan was *atheos* the negation of God *in privatio* or simply the absence of God. In that case, the greatest evil known would be death insofar as it implies a total annihilation of the ego and the sum of life experience as well as God and the known universe. Such a notion would, however, be both unsustainable if not inexplicable from a theological standpoint and regardless of any schoolboy notion of the absence of empirical evidence. Being was, accordingly, simply banished using the device of a dialectical logic where the metaphor of what is remains the paradox of Being. The redeeming premise was thus formulated as the *privatio boni*, where Evil is dialectically the absence of The Good. Dialectical negation, however, is not very convincing insofar as a substantiative assumes its negation as its complement and which is a tautological or self-predicating proposition. Obviously, the negation remains empty and without substance and hardly providing itself as a veritable complement.

Jung labored this point by declaring Satan and Evil are not simply negations of God and the Good but substantial in themselves and following the Kantian rule of Noumenon or thing in itself *(ding an sic)*. That would allow Good and Evil as proper complements. The notion is alarming if only it rendered the nature of dialectical reason as fallacious. This would, of course, alarm a traditional theologian as well as Hegel and later a Marxist Dialectical Materialist. In either case, a notion of the absence of something remained problematical as much as both good and evil as complementary somethings. What remained at large both theologically and then scientifically was a concept of nothing or nihilio as a pleroma of absolute vacancy and hence, as Aristotle understood it, as *ens in potentia* as the source of a pure and unconditioned potential previously more ironically alluded to by Plato as a receptacle or womb-place without previous impress, i.e., virgin, as noted in his *Timeaus*. The concept of "virgin," however, overlaps the principle of *nihilio.* or nothing, and its predicate as Pure potential. The latter, however, is the bugbear for all truth grounded in "empirical evidence."

The Boundless and Pure Potential

If you were an old Greek like Anaximander that which is without boundary is empty in the sense of devoid of eide or particular "elements." Yet, in a something out of nothing possibility a nothing is generated out of nothing. What is winnowed out *(apocrisis)* from the Boundless is without substance but the principle of *enantia* (opposites). This principle potentates an enantiadroma (the dynamics of opposites as the conflict or reconciliation of opposites). It was Empedocles who determined enantia concerned eide or substantial material "elements" (air, water, earth and fire) that paired up in the dynamic of enantia. In this sense, Anaximander's apieron (boundless) is a pleroma of pure potential devoid of differentiated elements (of matter).

On the other hand, "pleroma" in the Christian, neo Platonic and Gnostic sense was always full because its tradition could not abide the possibility of *nihilio ex creatio* (creation out of nothing) when it in fact indicated *nihil qua potentia*. Thus Plotinus found it necessary to provide a concept of *(steresis)*, the privatio boni, evil, or material reality, as simply the absence of the Good or better say- "dread" as they were fain to acknowledge it- the unthinkable notion of the Absence of God as not only Creator of all things but of Himself. Significantly enough, this tautological view does not contradict the Biblical account of Genesis where the first day of Creation is identical to the Greek Apieron and a concept of the irrepresentational pleroma of predisposition to form (*facultas praeformandi*) as apparently empty. The fact is; however, the philosophers were not addressing existential phenomena but a mode of thinking that could accommodate such predispositions and hence endorse a concept of Immanence.

Be it here reminded that the notion of the *ding an sich* and Kant's Noumenon are throwbacks to the Greek philosophical tradition of never assessing a phenomenon "right on" (*prosus*) and making a judgement accordingly. Philosophical explication came only through the eidos and its grasp of the eide that were already conceptual quantums that are neither phenomenal nor existential. The eide were thus the currency of authentic thinking and what today, qua Kant, we nominalize as the thing in itself and which is hardly an existential thing (of perception) "in itself" but as eide. Need it be added that "thinking" in its philosophical mode is impossible without such parsing of phenomenon in favor of an abstract conceptual unit (as eide or *ding an sich*) that as such are the materia of the eidos. I dare say that from hands on Alchemy to scientific empiricism the Greek method of thinking qua the eidos is totally irrelevant if not defunct in a current epistemology.

Thus, the thing in appearance must be distinguished from "Non-repr-esentational" and which I further cannot address simply because as a "Non" or negation of "what is" (*ti esti*) remains without substance and not grounded in *physis*. Indeed, it is a nothing qua negation but, accordingly, also qualified as potentia. This would put it in league with steresis and the privatio negation because its premise as *ens in potentia* defies the dialectic logic that is subject to a *circulus in probando* (tautology) or self-predication. For the Greeks, however, the only allowable tautology was the Ur or archai reality of *ti esti*, It is because it is grounded in the proto-hyle known as *ousia* (as essence, eidos or principle of matter) and by which the prima materia is essentially nihil. Aristotle, however, in his formulation of entelecheia identifies the state of pure nothing as equivalent to potentia whose necessity is he presence of "nothing." In that case, the paradox of metaphor is the essence of a metaphysical statement.

Jung arrived at his unwitting desecration of dialectical method by claiming Evil was something and not simply the absence of something else. The two notions were strangely overlapped except Jung had grounded the unus mundus in his idea of the prima materia derived in his vast study of alchemy. This, however, no more than reiterates second hand Aristotle's understanding of prima materia as a primal ousia or proto-hyle. The two concepts certainly had much in common, except the alchemy of Gehard Dorn that Jung followed had reified the prima materia as in fact a stone (Lapis). Did the stone, via its Alexandrian Arabic influence, replace the psyche and thus materialize it as the object of unconscious projection If such were the case it missed the point of Aristotle's prima materia by intruding the later Arabic Islamic preference for the stone in its Ka'aba at Mecca.

The void of Death thus prevailed as The Stone (or Lapis) and is in equivalence to what Jung called the unus mundus as noted by Gehard Dorn, the German alchemist. Dorn derived the idea of the unus mundus from Aristotle's prima materia who borrowed the concept in turn from the pre-Socratic physiologoi, Anaximander. Aristotle's version was, however, imported to Europe during the Arabic invasion of Spain and with it the practice of Alchemy. The original Aristotelian materia prima, imported by Alexander the Great to Egypt was therefore decommissioned as literally a stone or Lapis in the Arabic and then European practice of Alchemy. A directed materialism thus set the alchemical process for manipulation of physical substances losing sight, as such, of the prima materia as ousia or essence of matter. That would have to wait for the questions raised by Quantum Mechanics. Jung, however, fell hook line and sinker for this contra-Aristotelian view and no doubt overwhelmed by its European Alchemy exotic imagery and its syncretistic mish-mosh (*miscombroglio*) of religious and philosophical ideas that were part of a Gnostic tradition extending from ancient Egypt, Ptolomaic and Alexandrian Macedonianized proto-Aristotelian philosophy and finally its introduction to Europe by the Arabic and Jewish invasions of Iberia.

The Mercurious: Locked Up or Lazy

As the ultimate representation of matter, the Lapis was understood to conceal the elixir of transformation known as the Mercurious. The alchemical opus, therefore, concerned freeing the Mercurious from its embedment in the stone. This obviously corresponded to the Arabic idea of freeing a geni trapped in a bottle or in a lamp as a means of being granted three wishes. "Three" also indicates Hermes Trismigustus or Hermes thrice blessed. The "wish" for Dorn was, however, for his own unity with the stone that represented the archai or ur-stone as the one and original world or unus mundus: literally, an archetypus mundus and which likens to the unus mundus insofar as both are irreprsentable. This amounts to saying that in death qua the unus mundus such unity is achieved as a final perfection or "nothing" except one is predisposed to the idea of nothing as Aristotle's pure potential. Lost in such translation was the original idea characterizing prime or archai matter as apieron, or an infinite "without boundary" undefined mass as a kind of super atom preceding Creation and more recently known as the big bang and ensuing expansion of the universe. In its equivalence to Death or a nihil state, it also served as the material first cause. It thus took on representation of the more ancient symbol of the ever-spinning Uroboros or tail-eating serpent, which devours itself unto Lethe.

The only active quality of apieron was that it spun like a whirlwind or tornado from which were "winnowed out" (apocrisis) an active principle of opposites (enantia) that stood in contention one to another. It is here that a dynamic of opposites begins as a concept. It was this concept that became the fundamental of Jung's approach to psychology. Empedocles further defined the eide that emerged from this prima materia as the four elements: water, air, fire and earth. Eros was thus preconceived in its uninterrupted original state as "virgin:" or in extended analog, as apieron, the boundless as prima materia, later referred to by European alchemy as the unus mundus. It reappears more recently as a massless super atom preceding the big bang of creation. Such proto-hylic and original "matter" that already embodied the thanatos states was pitted against Strife (neikos) and its destructive intent.

Nothing as Something

On the other hand, "pleroma" in the Christian, neo Platonic and Gnostic sense was always full because its tradition could not sustain the possibility of nihil qua potentia, as indicated as the Aristotelian prima materia. Thus Plotinus found it necessary to provide a concept of (steresis), the privatio boni, evil, or material reality, as simply the absence of the Good or better say-"dread" as they were fain to acknowledge it- the unthinkable notion of the Absence of God as not only Creator of all things but of Himself. Significantly enough, this view does not contradict the Biblical account of Genesis where the first day of Creation is identical to the Greek *Apieron* (Boundless) and a concept of the irrepresentational pleroma of predisposition to form as apparently empty. How could what is void produce something. How could it not, according to Aristotle, since what is empty is so as the full measure of pure potential? The fact is; however, the philosophers were not addressing existential phenomena but a mode of linear thinking that could not accommodate such predispositions.

Be it here reminded that the notion of the ding an sich and Kant's noumenon are throwbacks to the Greek philosophical tradition of never assessing a phenomenon right on and making a judgement accordingly. Philosophical explication came only through the eidos and its grasp of the eide that were already conceptual quantums that were neither phenomenal or existential. The eide were thus the currency of authentic thinking and what today, qua Kant, we nominalize as the thing in itself and which is hardly a thing (of perception) but "in itself" as eide, a quantum of something thought rather than perceived. Need it be added that "thinking" in its philosophical mode is impossible without such parsing of phenomenon in favor of an abstract conceptual unit (as eide or ding an sich) that as such are the materia of the eidos. I dare say that from hands on Alchemy to scientific empiricism the Greek method of thinking qua the eidos is totally irrelevant if not defunct in a current epistemology, indicating "modern Man" as a technological genius is but an epistemologically unaware ignoramus.

Jung arrived at his unwitting desecration of dialectical steresis method by claiming Evil was something and not simply the absence of something else. Before this, however, the question was astoundingly re-evoked by an early advocate of Psychoanalysis, Sabina Speilrein in her thesis, Destruction as a Cause for Coming Into Being" (*Die Destruktion als Ursache des Wirdens*). Borrowing discreetly from his "psychotic" inspiratrix ("a talented psychopath who had a strong transference to me."[40]), Jung later formulated the relation in his idea of psychological transformation: where a virtual death must precede a "rebirth. Freud was also inspired by Sabina's simple formula in his notion of a "death instinct" or drive (*todestrieb*) in contest with Eros, as life drive. In all cases, the telos is directed for a condition of life after death insofar as the Resurrection of Christ and the promise of eternal life was not sufficient for such hypothetical intellectual meandering. It is as if to say, "I am going to design my own hereafter", a posture more familiar as the inflation of the personality. The problem here is that of a pretense to thinking and knowing rather than feeling and experience which is best left to Goethe's Gertrude.

Neglected in either case is the history of concept formation as the product of thinking and knowing. In the inability of the inflated personality to deal with the means only the ens remained in sight and which in a previous work I referred to as the masculine quest for the "final perfection" and the symbiotic relation of inflation and the death drive. My notion was in com999999999mon with Freud's *todestrieb* ("Death Drive").

In Jung's case it was materialized as the unus mundus as final unity and no less an ontological state of Death qua Nihil. Fraulein Speilrein, however, understood "coming into being," and however both Freud and Jung borrowed it, the pre-Socratic Anaximander 2500 years before had parented the idea in his concept of apocrisis, the "winnowing out" of opposites from The Boundless (apieron) or eternal state of being as an empty pleroma.

Yet, this premise of something out of nothing prevails to this day. The apocrisis would be herald to the death of apieron as forms in appearance came into being. That which was without limit or in effect nihil was literally the source of not simply the world of materiality but Being and in turn God and the Good and in general, that Which Is (Parmenides). In order to get on with the creation the state of nihil had to be "killed" and which amounts to the death of Death for the state of beings in appearance to arrive.

Death: Something or Nothing

The problem of creatio ex nihilio indicated creation as simply something out of nothing where the state of Death & co. remained as an invisible "something that is nothing" and with no place in a concept of being." From Jung's contrary idea that Evil was a substantive it would also follow that Death qua Evil was ontologically something as a state of being and not the agency of pure negation. That would allow it as a place to be following death. Hence, destruction and death were proposed by Fraulein Speilrein as the cause or source to being. Indeed, no sooner allow evil (qua Death) as something substantive and not a mere negation it enjoys being: ergo, Death as a state of being. In effect, Jung's abolishment of the privatio boni would infer a substantive life after death.

Astoundingly enough, the notion resembled the Teutonic Raganorok and Twilight of the Gods. The consequence of such a decisive and finalistic death of immortal gods and mortals was the creation of a new round of earthly and cosmic being. The instrument here was destruction and death and what later took form as a place or space called Hades. Aides was approximated to a state or "house" of death and indeed no more full than the unus mundus, i.e., both the house of death and the Unus as an empty pleroma devoid of time and space. It was, however, in equivalence to the Aristotelian prima materia as pleroma of pure and undefined potential, i.e., the anti-space of predisposition to form. Apparently, nothing represented potential as a futuristic what will be. Interestingly enough, the Teutonic cosmology included only the past and the present precluding as such a concept of potential and a temporal future. In the futuristic state, however, form is entirely irreprsentable, as would be the case for Jung's taxology of the archetype as no more than a predisposition to form, i.e., the archetype as nothing or a Hadean (Death) property.

In the more traditional sense, Hades as abode of Death became the standard Greco-Roman place reserved for non-material ghosts or shades. Even the Boundless (apieron) embodied only the opposites as a dynamic rather than material and in being elements. This would, of course, assign the complex of opposites to the ontological state of Death and, as such, to a tautological self-creation of opposites. It would amount to Death creating out of itself or in and by itself. The proposition would, indeed, violate the privatio boni and what was for centuries held *sui generis* by philosophers and theologians alike as an impropriety. Indeed, Jung's "little girl" patient, as Freud called Sabina, had dropped a hot potato in his lap. It later stimulated him to follow up Empedocles who went one step further than Anaximander: naming in kind, as in the Second Day of Creation, the coming into being of four elements that paired up as opposites: water/earth, air/fire. Jung, not to pass up a good opportunity, psychologically replicated this in his formulation of four fundamental psychological types: feeling/water, earth/sensation, air/thinking and fire/intuition. Such a reduction of material elements to psychological types is achieved without the full entelechy accounting for the generation of material elements from potentia to telos. That would leave the type theory as purely analytical and as such tautologically predisposed and without substance. That is, however, also the problem with Freud's Psychoanalytical as well as Jung's Analytical Psychology.Neither could rest their psychological premises as grounded in "empiricaL evidence except that of an analytically statistically kind. That, of course, does not preclude it as a form of praxis insofar as analyst qua Analyzant both are grounded in the premise of a psyche partitioned as both unconscious and conscious and whose entire versimultitude is regulated by a principle of the complexio oppositorum and which is not uncommon to any principle fostered b y the philosophers and alchemist of old Alexandria.Thus Jung is not far off in his poetic phantasm of the "dead written by Basilides in Alexandria, the City where East toucheth the West." and, of course, Jung was originally provoked by "the dead" in Sabina's notion of destruction (death) as the necessity of new being.

Freud was equally moved by the Little Girl's hypothesis, hardly aware that it equally coincided with the pre-classical culture hegemony of the Teutonic Destruction qua new being *Gotterdammerung*. In a radical turn of mind, he soon enough bypassed Eros in its limitation to nothing but sexuality. His *Beyond the Pleasure Principle* followed as a revised view of Eros. It was more generically assigned as "life drive" and what Freud equated with the original Platonic androgyny. In this form male and female are not differentiated but prevailed fused rather as a single ontology. The androgyny was a mythogenic attempt to render The Boundless and the unus mundus as ironically anthropomorphic, expressing the union of opposites as a bodily affair, just as Arabic alchemy reified the prima materia as in fact a stone as the mother of all material elements. This is also the principle regulating transgenderization.

The spherical androgynous being was, however, asexual and where genders opposites were indwelled as no more than predispositions to form. Rather than a unity it represents a fused or homogenized state of opposites that again recapitulates the boundlessness of the unus mundus and Anaximander's apieron. In all cases, a concept of The One included all as well as nothing and thus bypassing a concept of Zero. Yet, The One that precludes Two is a state of fusion of undifferentiated parts or simply a unity without parts. Only with Two is a unity (of one and Another) possible.

Apparently, unknown to Freud the Platonic androgyny was merely an extension of the Aristotle's prima materia and Gehard Dorn's unus mundus. More noticeable, however, Freud's todestrieb was in quick relation to the popular *Sturm und Drang* (storm and stress) German Romantic Movement. Sturm was distinctly related to "drive" or *trieb* thus suggesting it as an instinctual bursting out whereas Drang was related to regressive distress, e.g., mania qua depression. Such polar extremes cannot be spoken of as a state of unity but as the vibrating quick flux of fusion, of one opposite devouring the other. This also raises the question of whether the unus mundus was in fact a state of fusion rather than a unity as Jung claimed. This primal state referred to fusion rather than unity, and thus better related to the realms of Hades, Death, Satan and Evil that for all philosophical purposes remained as merely the insubstantive absence of Being. Such a notion would have ignored the imperative agency of Destruction and Death, something not neglected by either the pre-Socratic physiologoi, the Pythagorean influence from the North and their remote connection to the Teutonic *veltgeist*. It also somehow preoccupied Fraulein Speilrein no matter she was unschooled in such matters when she alarmed both Freud and Jung with her axiom of destruction as the necessity of new being.

As an ontological singularity the notion of the unus mundus was also derived by Gehard Dorn as not only a unity of being but, as with Sabina, both the archai and Eschaton of coming into being. The latter would relate it more to the apocrisis or winnowing out of the opposites. For Jung and his alchemical studies, it was a case of conflict of opposites and their final merging *(coniunctio)* as the unus mundus. For Martin Heidegger the process was abstractly translated in his *Zein und Seit* as a process of *dasein*, or beings thrown out into the world or realm of Time.

However, in either case merely replicated was the original notion of Anaximander's apocrisis. Only after the opposites arrived from the chthonian realm of Death was it possible to qualify them as essential material elements by Empedocles. Jung, following Sabina's premise did not miss the point that "Death and Destruction" were involved in such a "da-sein" and already pronounced in the Biblical account of Genesis as the First Day of Creation. There is no way of knowing whether Fraulein Speilrein was aware of this in her original paper. It was certainly an extension of a Goethean perspective. Apparently neither did Freud miss the point and thus altered his premise that *Eros Ist Alles* was not simply a matter of sexuality. For Goethe's Faust it was a case of gefuhl ist alles and which assimilated both Feeling and Eros as the subject of a generic life drive that Goethe generalized as simply "nature. He also claimed Nature as the ground for his poetic rather than philosophical efforts. It was reflected in Faust's definition of religion in terms of gefhul and the feminine approach to it. For the thinker and knower, however, religion was a dead issue insofar as feeling and experience was subverted by thinking, cogito ergo sum.

Apparently, quite the opposite was true for Sabina with her intuitive feeling. Freud, however, complemented this feeling/eros with the death-drive as the telos of stress and depression that was generic as the sturm und drang of the German Romantic Movement. This was obvious enough insofar as it would then literally go beyond the pleasure principle as the motivating trieb for sexuality, Eros qua Thanatos.

Herakleitos of Ephesus also suggested the erotic relation to death is not distinctly all sexual when he notes that Dionysus and Hades are one person. Reflecting on a feminine cult celebration, he notes: "For if it were not to Dionysus that they made a procession and sang the shameful phallic hymns, they would be acting most shamelessly. But Hades is the same as Dionysus in whose honor they go mad and keep the feast of the wine-vat."[41]

What saved the day for the pre-Socratic philosopher's moral righteousness was the "sameness" of Dionysus and Hades. It indicated the Eros/Thanatos two-in-one and its alarming personification as ambivalence, one the bottom side of the other. It revealed itself as a virtual *complexio oppositorum* by which the elements of such a dyad (Eros/Thanatos) are in conflict and yet in harmony. However, the overtly phallic attributes of Hades (Death) remain unseen, invisible, or hidden (lethe), as would be the case with Death, or place of the dead (Hades).

The Ideal *Complexio Oppositorum*

From Jung's alchemical view the two opposites must reconcile and ultimately unite. This perfect union by which life and death were joined was called the unus mundus (One World). For all purposes it is an analog for the afterlife and a state of immortality but postulated outside of a formal Christian meaning. What it retains, however, is the concept and image of Hades as the Devil but barring any explanation of the function of the greatest evil known as Death, Hades, Hell, and the underworld of the "maternal unconscious." The implication points to a phallic nature and a most archaically represented animus as in fact an immanence native to "Hell" but, more psychologically, as the indwelled animus of the maternal unconscious ironically offered in Jung's baby dream of the underground phallus.

On a lighter side for Herakleitos, "penis parades" were quite common in the ancient world as popular celebrations. In his Poetics Aristotle attributed the comedic form in drama as originating in such celebrations. The Hadean aspect was thus diminished in importance more so in view of popular ritual observances. The idea of Death and the underworld (chthonios) was, however, also cosmetically redressed in a modern secular Depth Psychology as simply the "maternal unconscious." This was, already mitigated by Goethe's "realm of the mothers" to which the old man Faust must suffer a confrontation in his pact with Mephistopheles who indeed was also combined as Eros/Thanatos. For the Teutonic cosmology, the "maternal unconscious" had its parallel as the underworld stream of Urtha that watered the World Tree, *Yggdrasil*. So long as the tree (*drus*) stood, Ragnarok was held at bay. Duplicated here was Jung's "tree of consciousness" that was felled with his break with Freud and consummated as what he referred to as his own "Confrontation With the Unconscious" noted in his Memoir.

One without Zero

The strange contradiction in Jung's one world unus mundus is that it begins as One and strangely neglects the Zero. The unit before One better accommodates not only the First Day of creation but also that of Death and nihil. Significantly, the ontology of Zero is not accounted for in Greek mathematics. It has its place, however, as a philosophical concept in the notion of apieron, the boundless, or that, which has no limit or boundary. In both cases time and space as "in this world" are precluded since "The One" posteriori follows the "Zero." Strangely enough Zero also had no place in the Roman number system but was included, along with alchemy, after its importation during the Arabic invasion of Iberia. Apparently, the Arabic view had misplaced its mathematical inclusion of Zero when it came to the empirical materialization that came with alchemical practice. Finality is thus summed up for Jung as matter in being (the unus mundus) but as the alchemical Lapis or stone.

Overlooked is the Zero State of Death as the prelude to The One of Being. Apparently, Jung was attempting to replicate the notion of a hereafter for which not only death is overcome but a principle of Evil. Death, of course, would be the greatest evil known, because unknowable, to mortals and, accordingly, represented by the animus as the less than mentionable Devil. Jung, however, ignores the identity of the Greatest Evil with Death and its various personifications of Satan and the Devil. Indeed not, since he did account for Zero (nihil) as the *ur-grund* for his unus mundus! Otherwise, the unus predicating mundus would be lapsed as *nihil mundus*.

Ironically, The One of Arabic alchemy although not accounting for zero was preferred in Jung's notion of the unus mundus. Strangely enough The One, as unus thus displaced the Zero, the latter of which better accommodated a concept of the prima materia as the immaterial potential of "no-thing, the apieron (as boundless or infinite) ousia, virtually a thing of eternity. But The One displacing nihil and the void amounted to a short cut for Jung because not accounting for a process of *apocrisis* or separating out from the center, the center being comparable to the unus mundus as void and what was included as the necessary dynamic for a process of entelechy or coming into being. The absolute void and the unus mundus were in fact the same and in the measure of Aristotle's prima materia to matter at its zero state, or that which is before it was. The problem with Jung's abbreviation and quick leap to the precepts of European alchemy was that the original idea of Aristotle's prima materia was immediately reified as a the Lapis, a literal stone that embedded or entrapped the potential of the Mercurious. This was the haptic or hands on influence of alchemical "lab work" which required a concrete material substance. On the way, however, the nature of the unus mundus as void was lost so that apocrisis was substituted for by the Mercurious as the dynamism of coming into being frozen inert in the heart of nothing. Missed, accordingly, was the Aristotelian necessity of nihilio as the only state that would define the pure and unconditioned potentia. Or, in Jung's language, "predisposition to form" but which he neglects to emphasise is in itself the primordial state of nothing but the pure potential. The omission is serious if for no other reason that the unus replaces the zero and thus skip-starts the process of entelecheia and as if an individuation process could take place with a "confrontation with the unconscious," or as otherwise said, the womb of the maternal unconscious as void or virgin. Hence Plato pre dated Aristotle by citing :receptacle" or Chora or *xwpa* as "without previous impress." The virgin or nothing state is thus early on understood as pre-requisite for *Be Coming* and stands in measure with Anaximander's previous notion of *apieron* or, "that which is without boundary," i.e., *The Boundless.* The concept thus remains intact for 500 years and from wherever Anaxamander cited the notion of the Boundless and thus original idea of the unus mundus but which in fact are neither "world" (mundus) nor unus but Zero. That Aristotle finally arrives to incorporate it in a theorem is stupendous enough. Its negation, however, would be to replace pure nothing or should we say "eternity" to so concrete a metaphor as a stone certainly amounts to taking the "roll" out of "rock!"

The stone thus served as the Arabic alchemical object analog for the maternal unconscious whose apparent state of nihil was precluded (and thus lost as an agency of pure potential). From a comparative standpoint such a perspective is crude and primitive if not a regression from the original Greek development commenced by the pre-Socratic *physiologoi*, such as Anaximander and mainly the Eleatic philosopher, Parmenides. The Eleatic view was later abstracted and refined by Plato but who may have balked at having his *xwpa* petrified.

In other words, the Arabic borrowing from Greek philosophy and materialized in their form of Alchemy was a corruption that was instituted in European alchemy all the way to Gehard Dorn's emphasis of inner spirituality rather than the alchemical empirical work and then Jung's psychological interiorizations. In all cases the problem was one by which nihilo was posed as the privation of being indicating nothing qua Death was without substance. It stood in contrast to the atavistic notion of stone and how it was considered since the pre-historic megalithic builders of Malta representing the maternal unconscious as a fixed permanence, as was the case with Egyptian pyramids and dolmens in general that embodied the space of Death. On the other hand, there was no reservation about comparing *The One* with a concept of wholeness, a saltus that would have alarmed a Greek philosopher. Wholeness presupposes parts, whether the whole is the sum of its parts or greater than the sum of its parts. *The One* as *the Zero* does no such thing. Both are empty, literally out of this world. Jung's focus on the unus mundus as One World thus infers a universe as a plenum other than the mundane mundus. From a meta-cosmological standpoint that may be the case for however we project the gnosis of the soul or Psyche into the universe at large and as if there were a knowable reality outside the Psyche and where the extra-psychic would be equivalent to the state of Death. And here we find out what the alchemist is really about: the quest for the final perfection called immortality or, from a more practical sensate standpoint, "Life after death" and which would, of course, presuppose God and eternal life as one and the same as *gnosis in eternus*.

PART THREE: THE FAUSTIAN ANIMUS

Jung, Faust and the Germanic Psyche

The most problematic aspect of the *animus archetypus* was explicitly demonstrated in Jung's baby dream of an underground phallus "rising up." It featured a giant erect penis standing in an underground chamber. He notes in his Memoirs the dream occurred when he was three years old. He then offers a most startling revelation: "...As a matter of fact, I did not say anything about the phallus dream until I was sixty-five. I may have spoken about the other experiences to my wife, but only in later years. A strict taboo hung over all these matters, inherited from my childhood."

In a more traditional interpretation suggested is the Devil himself rising in his bottomless pit. At worst, the image would satisfy the Johanine notion of the arrival of the anti-Christ and the End of Days. However, as an animus, it would be proper as an archetypal image to the feminine psyche if not a property of the maternal unconscious. As much is suggested insofar as it may pre-empt the concept of the animus as both a psychic and trans-psychic archetypal phenomenon. On the other hand, from a personal standpoint baby Jung may have dreamed his mother's undreamable psychism. From the suprapersonal standpoint however, the dream animus is on one hand the psychological contra-sexual soul image of the feminine psyche and simultaneously The Spirit in all its generality as *animus mundus*. Allowed, as such was the animus as specific not only to the feminine psyche but to that of the masculine as well. In the latter case, the male is indicated as a walking, talking animus, as it were, the nature of its active personality as given to Western Culture and whose norm is the inflation of the personality. In the former, it is psychologically limited to a feminine projection of the male image: the male from the feminine unconscious standpoint. Both aspects overlap no sooner their transpersonal commonality is considered. They do so, however, as a complex of opposites, on one hand drawn in their homogenous similarity, and on the other as trenchant antagonists by which the animus assumes the role of Spirit rather than soul (psyche) and thus active regardless of gender. It then assumes the role of agent to the conflict of opposites and what Jung posed as the alchemical problem of opposites and its final resolve in unity as the unus mundus.

The alarming late notice of Jung's baby dream, however, indicated that Jung himself was from early on gripped by this ambivalence. Yet, as he later in life admitted, his No. Two personality also included the ritual phallus that he dreamed as a child. It is, as such, quite the opposite to that of the wise old man Philemon, his transcendant spirit guide in the form of an elderly winged man who appears substituted for the "shamelessly ambitious old man," Faust. It did, however, express the Faustian fantasy of the old man of seeking wisdom. It equally expressed the erotic adventures of Faust in his bargain with the Devil. Surely, the little boy Jung was not versed in Goethe, no matter how much he later toyed with the idea that his great grandfather was the bastard child of the Greatest of German philosophers and poets. Jung's personality No.2 apparently had more to do with an aspect of the Collective German psyche where he "...felt himself in secret accord with the Middle Ages, as personified by Faust, with the legacy of a past which had obviously stirred Goethe to the depths. For Goethe too, therefore-- and this was my great consolation-- No. Two was a reality. Faust, as I now realized with something of a shock, meant more to me than my beloved Gospel according to St. John. There was something in Faust that worked directly on my feelings[42].

Such feelings were, however, the radical complement of his thinking and knowing by way of his No. One personality. Was, in fact, No. Two urging him toward the Faustian *gefuhl is alles* and the thinking man's world of No.1? Here the early forced Christianization of Germany and its lingering resentment asserts itself: "John's Christ was strange to me, but still stranger was the Savior of the other Gospels. Faust, on the other hand, was the living equivalent of No. Two, and I was convinced that he was the answer which he had given to his times." such yearning immediately pushes Jung back from the Christian event to what was going on in Alexandria and its introduction to the Aristotelian theorem of entelecheia in the immediate following of Alexander, Ptolomaic Egypt and the beginning of applied alchemy. Jung never mentions this but it may have been subliminally epigenetically embedded in his psyche and emerging not in his professional and scholarly work but as his fantasy of the dead speaking from Alexandria. The only tangible clues he would have was in his intense interest in alchemy which was already second and third hand evolved from Thomas Acquinus, to Paracelsus and then Gehard Dorn. All were in the Aristotelian tradition emerged from Alexandria to the Continent through Spain to Germany. Dr Marie-Louise von Franz approaches this her Study of the aurora and Thomas Acquinas but, like Jung only briefly accounts for Aristotle and his compatriot, Alexander and who, as such. would account for Jung's speaking dead of Alexandria: that is to say "dead" because "unconscious" for both Jung and von Franz. Such limited mindedness may be accounted for because their Germanic priorities took precedence over the Alexandrian event and which did not include the Germanic culture of the time which, as a non urban society was still at odds with Rome attempting to "tame" and thus colonize Gaul. On the other hand, to reach further back, it may be understood that Illyria (modern Albania) along with Macedonia, Thrace and Sparta were derived from a Proto-Germanic or Teutonic and Nordic people that included all of Scandinavia. After all, Homer's heroes invading Illium were cited as Dorians and Aachains stemming from the North, a tradition that lasted to the expeditionary predispositions of "Vikings" whose ancestors sailed down the Danube in their flat bottomed, double-ender long boats into the Pontus Euxine and all the way to what is now Kiev and then north to found European Russia. Such was also the genetic background of both Alexander and Aristotle. That is precisely the position Jung takes for his resistance to Christianity that was eventuated and evolved in Alexandria. As such, Christianity may be counter to one of Jung's speaking dead of Alexandria.

Apparently Jung was not at home with Christianity even as his father was a Christian Minister: "This insight was not only comforting to me, it also gave me an increased feeling of inner security and a sense of belonging to the human community." By "human community" he intended as "German community" as if *Deutschland Uber Alles* were to be his single rule: "I was no longer isolated and a mere curiosity, a sport of cruel nature. My godfather and authority was the great Goethe himself. [43]"

Did he imply by this his identification with Faust and his pact with the Devil and as if without Christianity *der devil ist uber alles?* Implicitly, the realm of Satan and Germany are the same indicating that Germany and Death, the infinite night, were equally so. Mirrored here is the conflict between Jung's No. 1 and No. 2 personalities. It is here worth noting that Jung's No. One extraversion was early on enjoyed serving Freud and his Psychoanalytic Empire.

Hades and the Animus

The animus as Spirit would then locate the ambivalent definition of animus in Goethe's Faustian terms: as the more extraverted male ego and its intrigue if not persona identification with the devil or Mephistopheles. But this immediately surfaces Jung's inferior (because not developed) No. Two personality first voiced in his childhood and associated with the underground phallus of his childhood dream and by which Death and Catholic priests appeared as of one fabric. Along these lines the animus is cast in the image of Hades, the Lord of Death, and which is replicated for Goethe as Mephistopheles, also a Lord of Hell and the infinite night, Hades or Death. But, Faust also has at his erotic disposal all womankind, from Helen of Troy to comely small town Gretchen. He is, indeed, easily personified in archetypal measure as the ever-ready phallus of Jung's baby dream but only after it has risen to disport itself in the mortal realm of the feminine presence. It emerges, accordingly, in the person of Jung's No. One personality and by which No. Two serves as its unconsciously motivating shadow side. Here, of course, I am using Jung's own analytic perspective to define him, more so it employs what he so strongly embraced as the enantiadromia of opposites. The ambivalence at once indicates the Hadean animus as simultaneously endowed with the power of generation as well as that of death and destruction. The underground phallus was as if postured to rise from its confinement in the Bottomless Pit of Hell and Death and to which Goethe gave notice as the Devil's confrontation with Faust.

As early as 1919 Jung correlated this underworld monster with the "blonde beast...prowling about in its underground prison, ready at any moment to burst out with devastating consequences.[44]" As with Nietzsche he was referring to the German zeitgeist, an animus mundi that was confined underground and like the alchemical Mercurius in all its energic potential to objectify itself with no less "devastating consequences." In Jung's case such devastation was anticipated in his traumatic "confrontation with the unconscious[45]" Soon after he parted with Freud.

In his three-year-old baby dream, a prophetic element was somehow epigenetically stamped during his infancy or before. Such were the rumblings from chthonios that troubled his No. One extraverted personality but channeled and sublimated as such into his need for young mistresses and a career of accomplishment in the field of Freud's Psychoanalytic. Both were served by the inflation of the young Jung as the up and coming Crown Prince of Freud's Psychoanalytic.

The immanence of the phallic animus image is especially problematical when understood as the ground covered in the early days of Psychoanalysis when Freud and Jung enjoyed a father and son relationship. During that time Jung followed Freud's notion of the primacy of sexuality. It was only later, after Jung's intimate affair with one of his own early patients ended and he simultaneously parted with Freud that he was able to more definitively formulate his concept of the animus: as the functional contra sexual agent of the feminine psychology. For practical therapeutical purposes, it was more often presented in either benign terms, or as the projected qualities of the negative masculine nature. It sometimes appeared as a gentle old man of wisdom (Philemon) and other times as a nasty and disagreeable fellow represented by the moody old man Faust in his quest for ur-wisdom. This was also the case with Goethe himself and then the No. One personality of Jung that required a"confrontation with the unconscious," meaning a passing psychosis and dissociation of ego-consciousness and all that was Jung's No. 1 personality.

In its negative venue the animus is thus easily accepted as the chronically given familiar but unpleasant personality of the male in search of final perfection, something definitively demonstrated in Ingmar Bagmen's film, Wild Strawberries and no less from an introspective woman's standpoint. In Jung's case this was later represented as the unus mundus that would realize in substance the integrated unity of his two personalities as his No. One extravert and his No. Two introvert. Not accounted for, however, was the Zero that predicates One but which marks itself as Jung's "confrontation with the unconscious" and his psychosis that followed his split with Freud.

No parlor game was this with Faust probing Goethe's Realm of the Mothers but an unmediated confrontation with the maternal unconscious. Surviving this, Jung's full "thinking" power was brought to bear in his masterpiece work, *Psychological Types*.

Virgins Galore!

After surveying Jung's memoir, *Memories, Dreams, Reflections* and the plethora of more recent biographical treatments of Jung, it became apparent that, if only euphemistically, the man's genius was compounded with a most devilish personal reality. It appeared to slavishly replicate the figure of Goethe's Faust who, in pact with the Devil proceeded to indulge a plethora of women, a virtual swarm of anima figures in the flesh (and for the flesh). Aside from Jung's first love and wife Emma, he Faust-like enjoyed a small coterie of crypto-mistresses composed essentially of very young ladies. They were or had been his patients: e.g., Sabina Speilrein who was followed in turn by Antinonia (Toni) Wolff and then the more mature and scholarly than erotically involved ladies such as Dr. Marie-Louise von Franz and then Frau Aniela Jaffee, his secretary who co-authored his memoir, *Memories, Dreams, Reflections.* Von Franz, who was the gifted scholar of them all finally met Barbara Hannah, a British painter who was characterized as a "gawky" woman with bad teeth, was a lesbian "who later shared her life and home with Marie-Louise von Franz, did not disclose that she had fallen madly in love with Toni Wolff, who did not return any emotion beyond professional friendship."[46] Regardless, or because of, such convoluted relationships all were in deep transference with Jung and his devilish appeal, what appeared to suggest either overt or crypto (unconscious) love affairs compounded in their awe of the man, or the man as animus *extraordinaire*, Faust qua Philomen, but dressed in redness.

Jung, as such, thus performed as an animus that proved irresistible from a woman's unconscious standpoint. Was Jung aware that his underground "rising up" phallus, remembered from a childhood dream, was the animus of the once virgin Queen of Death? Would that account for his prolific need for transference traffic with very young Ladies who arrived as his patients? Apparently, his person(a) provided an animus image of the male as a semi-divine *ur-bild* or archetypal figure by which transference and love were combined as a form of worship by which the woman is mesmerized into submission. This, of course, was not so unusual in terms of actual love relationships not, at least, until after Freud's sexual revolution when sexuality was less considered in transcendent terms but more by and of the flesh where the spiritual or intrapsychic effect was diminished.

Soon enough, such affairs became more public and were no longer confined as the Original Sin of the world parents in the Garden of Eden. The extra-marital excesses of public figures such as Presidents Jack Kennedy or Bill Clinton hardly ruffled the political feathers of a voting public collectively in transference with them and for whom a "piece of ass" was no more than that, a purloined Big Mac with greasy bacon.

What captured the imagination, however, was the counter-transference enjoyed and suffered by Jung himself. He certainly did not encourage a dilemma that, by this time of the second millennium, has become a source for vicarious public entertainment. My original premise thus shifted its focus from the animus itself, insofar as in Jung's counter-transference he noticeably served as the projected animus to all the "love-lady" patients, by way of the instrumentation of transference. But, unlike in the contemporary moment, he was not feministically indulged as simply a phallic stud, or a Bubba at large in his private office. Indeed, he became a "star," not in the fashion of Freud as an ideological sexuality liberator but in the growing concern for spiritual enlightenment in a world suffering disenchantment with religion and utterly compromised by both a new materialism and indulgence in Christophobic political doctrines. Such culture disruptions were in fact the archetypal role of Zeitgeist, the Spirit, and the Paraclete that comes as a destroyer and equally cast as the psychological animus rising in the individual and collective consciousness. In that may we recognize the "negative animus" whom is more of the devil's party and the Spirit or animus mundi gone morbid? Here Jung fit the bill and where the unconscious No. 2 personality was in the embrace of an unholy Lord Jesus, in effect serving as a personified animus figure for all women who passed his way with, perhaps, the exception of his wife, Emma. She had to assimilate his harem unto herself or integrate the negative animus as a component of (her) Self.

Jung's greater appeal was for women whose animus conflicts were exceptional and where the animus had so entirely overwhelmed the persona to the effect of a virtual transgenderization. In that case, he conveniently recommended a proper Lesbian affair. He appropriately indulged wealthy American women who promoted him financially and otherwise. On one hand Jung was equally disenchanted with the secularizing of Spirit, and on the other, responsible for further reducing it to a psychological causality and a pretense to scientific empiricism. In either case the problem was mitigated as he himself expressed a persona possessing him, through Philemon, as the world spirit, veltgeist and zeitgeist. He could thus play his persona both ways, from the ultra spiritual to the hyper carnal in the alternating current of No. 1.And No. 2 personalities.

Contrary to his No. One Personality's good reason for maintaining a scientific propriety, there lurked in his work a driving concern for religious images and motifs, a contradiction that he justified by insisting all such spiritual phenomena was reducible to a psychic and psychological source, precluding, as such, any thread leading to a metaphysical or transcendental reality. Yet, Jung and his work maintained, if only in pretense, a transcendental veneer. The spiritual aspect was, of course, closer linked to both the thanatic and erotic aspect of the animus. He, accordingly, found himself spread-eagled between the science of psychoanalysis and a phenomenologically reconditioned metaphysic and its treatment of Eros and Thanatos. These two aspects were in contest with one another and by which he grounded his view in a *principium oppositorum* and enatiadromia by which opposites or complements could automatically switch places. Such ambiguity was, of course, by necessity in the service of his two personaities that could not enjoy the duplexity of paradox and metaphor.

The Animus of the Anima

Less abstractly and more fundamentally was the ambivalence derived in his sustained belief that his life experience was expressed by two distinctly polar personalities. As one of the pioneers in the study of dementia praecox, as schizophrenia was called at the time, he himself was his own prime "patient" more so he was split as if both a womanizing Faustian figure and a dedicated man of science or alternately, a faithful husband and father, his compulsions as philanderer, notwithstanding. Consequently, woman in the flesh composed of his female patients received the projection as his endopsychic anima: literally the animus of the anima, as the man himself, a most supraordinate animus figure. Inflation notwithstanding they were, accordingly, equally a sources of inspiration and wisdom for him. If, Jung may have never included the function of anima as a primary concept in his Analytical Psychology and which followed the example of Parmenides and his goddess Aletheia, the "unconcealed" as source of Truth!

In a psychic exchange the women in his life served Jung as his agencies of inspiration whether in bed, in dialogue or with pen in hand, by which his intuition was availed a long leash. It didn't take much insight to realize that a man's genius was contingent to his relation with the feminine estate of the *femme inspiratrix*, more traditionally if not politely referred to as a man's "muse." For myself, on h other hand, as both a painter and poet, a problem arouse because its was quite apparent that if in psychic fact an anima was at large that demanded much intense introspection---especially that I was privy to Jung's understanding of the anima---the question of whom or what was the agency by which my creative work came into being? Did I, myself, appear merely subaltern to this anima In my long interest in Jung and the psychological approach of Analytical Psychology, I accepted the possibility that it was urgent to, come what may, integrate this anima in the greater whole of my personality in a psychological process of individuation and expression of the self.

Good enough! But did an ontological totality precede me and thrust me prematurely into a going beyond the limits of my reach? Was this also the case with Jung and his personality ambivalence or any man who dares follow his nose down the uterine way to Chthonian Hell? Soon enough, I found myself grounded in the paradigm of Jung and his personal myth. I realized he, along with all men, was preconditioned by the maternal animus supporting *uberman* as a spirit personified, the better to downcast "the woman" as a de-spiritualized quantum. Indeed, the more an inflation elevated the ego as The One the anima was limited to a dyadic nature with the devil as her cohort. In my own trans-Atlantic transference to Jung and then brief correspondence with him, I found myself involved in an intense inflation with the more than personal concepts and images provided by Jung that intruded on those of my own in my creative experience as a painter and poet.

Consequently, I experienced a waning interest in the exotic images of alchemy that enchanted Jung and preferred to enjoy my own variety of creatively generated primordial forms. Neither was I prepared to reduce my own spontaneously created images to explanation using Jung's approach to dream interpretation by way of their commonality with the archetypal ground of alchemy: e.g., Jung using the dreams of physicist Wolfgang Pauli, and correlating them with the archetypal residues of alchemical images and ideas. I began to feel sorry for Pauli who was already torn between his native Roman Catholicism and at the other end, his work as the prize winning physist who predicted the actuality of the neutrino as a most elusive nuclear particle. I am unaware if mention was ever made that the neutrino had a psychoid archetypal reality insofar as it performed like Hermes and its coming and going, now here, now there, but who is also the prototype to the binarius and the twoness of the Devil. No doubt eluding Pauli was his Hermetic function or endopsychic perception (intuition) further bogged down in Jung's obsession for the alchemy that was limited to Gerhard Dorn and his particular milieu. It is with this in mind that I began to sense my own intuition imposed upon by my transatlantic inflation with Jung and his work. Also apparent was how the transference relation induced inflation, in effect, elevating me beyond the means of my given personality: the inability of the inflated personality to deal with the means only the *ens* remained in sight and which in a previous work I referred to as the masculine quest for the "final perfection" and the symbiotic relation of inflation and the death drive:[47] As much as I sought to draw my creativity exclusively from myself the faster I literally approached a "dead-end." In Jung's case thanatos was already given form in the company he kept, identified with Faust and the realm of binarius, the "Twoness" of the Devil and its enclosure in the "realm of the mothers" and archaic feminine. But this was par for the course in the alternating current of his No. 1 and No. 2 personalities that were actualized at his threshold of consciousness. The dilemmas of duplexity had not openly effected me, or at best did not problematically seem to until my senior years and precipitated by the sudden rush of memory of my near death experience while at sea: a memory long forgotten of an incident when as a 19 year old merchant seaman the troopship to which I was committed as crew, blew up, in the North Sea, and was ordered abandoned. In the process of lowering a lifeboat, I nearly perished. Suddenly, and more recently, a door was sprung open to me and for the simple reason that the vessel was named the "Alexander" and where even as I had once put into the city of Alexandria aboard another ship, I of late ran head on into Jung's "*The Seven Sermios to the Dead written by Basilides in Alexandria, the City where East toucheth the West*" My shock doubled in a coincidence with Alexander the Great and founder of Alexandria on an Egyptian shore. He was in fact an ancient kinsman of mine insofar as my paternal heritage included Albania but which were known in antiquity as *Epirote* and *Illyria* and the birthplace of Alexander and his sister Cleopatra. Aristotle was also from the same area. It seems that the Twoness in all its duplexity as the devil's workshop was now upon me and I could now actively empathize rather that identify with Jung's particular wrestling with the Dark Angel whose number was archetypally up as Two, the Binarius.

My ship, as coincidence would have it also had two separate Identities, the one I knew as the troopship, The "Alexander" and its more opaque background as the SS Amerika, built and in service from 1905 to 1917 for the German Hamburg Amerika Line. Interned during WWI it was made to fly the stars and stripes as a US troopship and by WWII was "Alexanderized" as the USAT E. B. Alexander, named after a US Army General (and not Alexander the Great). The serendipitous word coincidence, however, relocated the name in my own Illyerian back yard, Alexander the Great qua Alexandria.

Something Out of Nothing

Thus began my preoccupation with what was in common with Freud's *todestrieb* ("Death Drive"). The morbidity of the subject was, however, mitigated by Jung's correlation of "Death" with a hardly materialized, but out of this world *unus mundus*, representing a final unity and no less an ontological state of Death. But the unus mundus was also predicated as qua *Nihilio ex Creatio* or, in effect, something out of nothing. From my imagical standpoint this could only mean: *The One as Being devoured of its parts (ontos) assimilated to extinction and no longer differentiated.* For Plato, I thought, this would have amounted to a catastrophe until I came upon his *hyperousia* and what transcended further The One but s the immovable Good or summum bonum. Nevertheless, I was not sure and the entire premise began to trouble me as much as my memory of abandoning a sinking ship. Now I was in deep trouble and there was only one thing to do: save the ship from sinking (which I actually helped do) by calling out my Reserves and response to my training as a seaman. In my new confrontation, this meant putting aside my poet's quill, paintbrushes, and donning my thinking cap. Accordingly, I knocked on the door of Aristotle and the Alexandria where his entelecheia became a premise for alchemy. But scuttled again, the philosopher turned out to be another ancient compatriot of mine and, like his pupil, Alexander, hailed from the far Western end of Macedonia, now called Albania. Indeed, he was also an Epirote! I was hindsighting my own beginning as if it were the end, supposing the past was easier to manipulate than future. Or that in the luxury of enjoying two personalities life is a closed book of complementarities, a *coincidentia oppositorum* now fit only for an old man straddled between beginning and end.

Couched in the wisdom of senility it is possible to enjoy the privilege of living in the before and after now. I cannot, however, pretend to know the optimum circumstance of living two lives fostered by two personalities or however it may insult a right thinking mono-minded sycophant to have both a wife and a mistress at the same time. This is especially true until one gets too old to see his dream walking or navigating at sea when Merman and Mermaid are not parted but go to sea without a ship. And if as much was for boys at sea as seamen who go to sea on ships, such as it was for me, some sixty-five years ago, urgent recall is now demanded before I put in to the other side and drop anchor for the last time and commit the greatest

Evil of all, the climax of mortality. Barring, however, a more youthful intellectual pretense, imperatively spiced with salty sea vernacular, it must right on be declared that a disturbing memory recall did not begin until after I was less physically indulged, and all in all more introspectively detained. Finally arrived in such mood, recall reached critical mass when I became for the first time in my life utterly and unreasonably concerned for a certain maritime disaster long put aside. Why now, would I measure and fathom with the plumb line of memory what enjoyed its privacy at the hoary bottom of Lethe. Yet, reclaim it as one must if only as an Old Salt's sea story with much excess added baggage that memory cannot ignore. A ship cannot go to sea without the proper ballast or it will bounce on every sea-swell like a fickle woman on a lumpy mattress.

With such advisory I proceeded anticipating a mix of "sea stories" accumulated during a brief three years spent at sea at the close of World War II, as well as some land acquired reminiscing from here, there and abroad. The truth of the matter is the first person involved is a personality apart from anyone of my common acquaintance and a cosmos apart from myself in the here and now. He is more a novelty for inspection or, at best, an attempt to understand a ghost not yet arrived. That perhaps is the motive for writing about the him who was me and whose ghost occupies only the vaporous time and space of a future embedded in memory. It is, however, even more wonder that this fellow is more often too brazen for my present temperament to entertain. His foreign personality that is apparently much concerned to get to know me, if for no other reason but to establish some reconciliation. Nevertheless, as the voice of my dead seagoing other he (it) now addresses me in French to spare my feelings: Ja Accuse!

It is, of course, not unusual that the lot of us enjoy or suffer two personalities that each alternate in time as an immediate persona reality which, if crowded at once and at the same time to fill that persona, may outcome in an uncomfortable disturbance. The risk, however, is worth it or forever shun that other of oneself, especially if they come, for whatever their reason, knocking and "would you, Sir or Madam, let me in." Aye, but only if you are from Alexandria and wake me up in voice as the dead.

Jung's Alexandria.

The bugbear of acausal coincidence, if there was such at the time, involved in the last analysis, much to do about nothing, except, of course, my happening to later intimate concern for Jung's *Sermons to the Dead* so that all that the events had really in common was the subject of The Dead and Death. And that, of course is gained only in retrospect and for my intrigue with Jung's peculiar indulgence in composing a mystic tome bylined as *The Seven Sermons to the Dead written by Basilides in Alexandria, the City where the East toucheth the West.* Was he "psyching" this or merely repeating an historical fact by which Eastern Persian is thought joined in synthesis with Western Hellenism?

As a result I continued my interest in Alexandria and not only because I had happened to have sailed as crew aboard a ship named "Alexander" but in first voyage at sea sailed aboard a vessel that in fact stopped at the Egyptian city. The name and coincidence intrigued me if only both the city and the ship enjoyed in common a long and variegated past. The ship, originally German was naturalized as American when interned during WWI and had many adventures and misadventures as a wanderer on the high seas. The City in kind was recently summed up for me in a review I read about the English writer Lawrence Durrell who spent much time in Alexandria and published four linked novels set in the City, called the *Alexandria Quartet* where he characterizes the city as: "Five races, five languages, a dozen creeds" that the reviewer noted, "If anything that understates the case. Arabs and Jews, Greeks and Italians, French and British, Armenians and Turks jostled together. Between the mosques and synagogues could be found the churches of Copts and Maronites, Chaldeans and Melchites, and all the many varieties of Orthodox and Catholic."[48]

A comparison of the ship to the city, however, came into play with Jung linking Alexandria with the dead and death and which immediately drew the conclusion that both the City and the Ship were ghosts. This was because in retrospect and further research I had taken to calling The Alexander "my Flying Dutchman" and for no other reason that it was a wanderer in time with a career at sea extending from 1905 to 1958. Reckoning the life of an Ocean Liner that is indeed an eternity. The story of the flying Dutchman had roots in an old Dutch legend that extended back to the German preoccupation with the story of the wandering Jew which immediately brought back to mind Jung's Philemon as a kind of Elijah and his relation to Salome who is directly involved with the Wandering Jew, also known as Ahasverus or Buttadaeus.

The linkage qua coincidences was beginning to trouble me especially recently when going through some old family documents left to me by my mother I came across something I had never seen before, my Baptismal Certificate. It was dated a few days after I was born documenting the Catholic ritual, which took place at St. Catherine's Church of Alexandria in Brooklyn, N.Y. It was all getting to close to home for me, as it were, personalized in a most disturbing coincidental way. St. Catherine of Alexandria was venerated during the Fifth Century, especially in the Orthodox Church for her martyrdom as a learned young virgin, persecuted by an infamous Roman Emperor. Seeing how much of my work focused on the nature and meaning of The Virgin, whether as Persephone Parthenos or the Virgin Mother Maria, the Baptismal revelation scored on two counts, recapitulation, again of Alexandria and my soft spot for the nature of Divine Virgins, notwithstanding the remoteness of the virgin nature for the risqué Salome. Jung's allusion to the blindness of Salome may be a reference to her once upon time virginity. In any case, there is, significantly enough, some resemblance of Elijah with Ahasverus as well in the overlapping of Woton and the *Ewige Jude* . Both are wanderers and which for German legend linked them to Woton. On the other hand, the alchemical Hermes also intrudes here and all of which give metaphor, if only superficially, to the Hermetic tradition of internalization of the alchemical opus and process. Appropriately enough, Jung's fantasy took Philemon beyond the wisdom embodied in the figure of Elijah. This in turn would transcend, or neglect, for Jung the relation of Elijah to both the Wandering Jew and Woton, the restless "wild huntsman" Teutonic god raging as the horrific sound of the wind in the tall pines of the Black forest, and who Jung accordingly cited as the blonde beast in anticipation of the catastrophe of a Wotonized Third Reich.[49]

Woton was, of course, the mythogenic figure serving as the counter-image or anti-Christ representing the resistance to the process of Christianization of Germany. The anti-Christ notion would accommodate the Wandering Jew who was doomed by Jesus for taunting him as he faltered carrying the cross for his execution and which the two figures in common resistance to Christ, even as they were in an ethnic and mythogenic sense, miles apart. The Germanic Woton, however, would include in the ancient Teutonic religion, Ragnarok and the death of the gods and end of the world, a climax that was equivalent to the destiny of the Wandering Jew destined to re-encounter Jesus at his second coming at the End of Days or, as in the German case, world's end. Germans and Jews were thus mated from the start in each their cosmological destiny. ,

Jewish legends about Elijah, nevertheless, abound in the *Aggadah*, which are found throughout various collections of rabbinical literature, including the Babylonian Talmud. This does not merely discuss the life of Elijah, but has created a new history of him, which, beginning with his death and which ends only with Days End and the close of the history of the human race. Yet, in such closure, following, no less, Sabina's *Die Destruktion als Ursache des Wirdens* (destruction leads to new being), suggesting in such a death there will occur a palingenesis, a coming again of being.

Again, the motif of the Wandering Jew is the basis of later legends and by which Elijah was not only the precursor of the Messiah. He was also zealous in the cause of God, and Elijah as the helper in distress. There are three leading notes struck by the *Aggadah*, endeavoring to complete the Biblical picture with the Elijah legends and by which his career is extensive, colorful, and as varied as that of Ahasverus and both of whom appear the world over in the guise of a beggar and scholar.

As proto-Faustian Seer, however, he had his Helen in the figure of Salome who served not only as his inspiratrix in their two thousand-year sojourn to Days End but was enjoyed, throughout the epic, for his erotic pastime. The overlap here, is that, although not mentioned by Jung, I suspect she served as much for his Philemon. The mystery further eludes transparency and thickens by something, which Jung avoids: that both Elijah and Ahasverus are further duplicated, however eponymously, in early German legends of the story of Faust, especially Goethe's Faust. Since the hubris of Faust, preoccupied Jung it is not so strange that he uses his Philemon as the redemption and transcendence of Faust. This also served to achieve the same for Elijah. Neglected by Jung, in any case, is the figure of the Wandering Jew. Nevertheless, even worse, Woton, remains without redemption for Jung. Yet, as much is implied in the earlier German assimilation of Woton as not only the Wandering Jew but also much later as Faust who bargains with Mephistopheles, the agent for Death (or Satan).

It is inferred but not spelled out by Jung that Faust is transfigured as Philemon. Yet, in old German legend, Woton, or Odhin, is transformed as the Wandering Jew and on one night in the year may rest, no less on a plow or harrow, and by which both Woton and the Wandering Jew are absolved. This takes place on Shrove Tuesday when all sins should be absolved, even for Woton, or Odhinn, the wild huntsman, known as Hackelberg who like a fierce wind pours through the forest, killing all in its path. But although no longer in league with the Wandering Jew both are relieved of their sins on Shrove Tuesday Woton remains as the pariah anticipated by Jung where he remains, like his other as the Jew, a restless wanderer who creates unrest and stirs up strife, here, now there, and works magic. Christianity soon changed him into the devil. Yet, Jung gives no account here that it was on the Christian celebration of Shrove Tuesday when both Woton and the Wandering Jew were forgiven. This slight avoids the issue that Jung's hermeneutic psychologizing of the Christian event marks him somewhat unsympathetic to Christian values and where there is no room for forgiveness and where absolution is provided instead by a horn helmeted Philemon, shade of his battle axer Wotonic ancestors who do not absolve sins but fly them away like Philemon until disappeared in the wild blue yonder as so much ritual funerary incinerated ashes. Between the fantasy and the actuality, an archetypal commonality prevails so that neither may preclude the other and whose only explanation lies in the phenomena of synchronicity and its psychoid reality where the archetype serves simultaneously in both areas simultaneously. More modestly can be accounted for as a "fate pattern" or heimarmene. Short of that both the Jews and their fate in the Third Reich are predicated as a projection rather than an actuality and may explain away the recent shiloah of Germany's Jews as if to diminish the impact the New and Old Testaments provided for early Germans. At any rate the coincidence of anti-Semitism with the reawakening of Woton is a psychological subtly that may be worth mentioning. It is thus all a minimal case of coincidence that early on forgiveness of both The Wandering Jew and Woton is put aside and which stands in the measure of the American, French and Bolshevik Revolutions as a renewed post-Roman anti-Christian culture mood.

The American separation of Church and State was thus a precaution that the New World nation would never succumb to pre-Reformation Papal Christianity. This mood, of course, was equally expressed in the Psychoanalysis of Freud and the Analytical Psychology of Jung by which the spiritual estate and religious experience could be reduced to tautological psychologism and in both Goethe and Jung's case, God is no more than defined according where feeling is everything and nothing more than a feminine preoccupation.. Christ is then replaced by Faust who in his commerce with the Devil (Mephistopheles) is related to Woton and the Wandering Jew who mocked Jesus on his way to execution. Accordingly, the Judaeo Christianizing of post-Roman Germans and the meaning of Shrove Tuesday are undone concerning both Woton and the *Ewige Jude*.

Certainly then, the redeeming figure for Jung is not Jesus the Jew but a reversion by Jung to the overall Germanic mythologem that is recapitulated for him in his fantasy:

> At Bollingen I am in the midst of my true life, I am most deeply myself. Here I am, as it were, the 'age-old son of the mother.' That is how alchemy puts it, very wisely, for the 'old man,' the 'ancient,' whom I had already experienced as a child, is personality No. 2, who has always been and always will be. He exists outside time and is the son of the maternal unconscious. In my fantasies, he took the form of Philemon, and he comes to life in Bollingen.[50]

Return to Alexandria

The fantasy that took place in his stone built fortress-like Bollingen retreat represented the turning point in his life: where he must redeem his No.2 introverted personality that he "already experienced as a child" and commence a new field of personal involvement and research. Accordingly he was at the climax of a stupendous transformation and what commenced his second half of life during which he became intensively involved in his investigations of alchemy and his crowning masterpiece, *Mysterium coniunctionis* and all of which may be marked as his "Return to Alexandria," where alchemy had its origin. His previous erotic compulsions with young mistresses now turned toward an authentically internal anima figure, a seductive *La Belle Juive* of Alexandrian alchemy notably pioneered as the Jewess, Maria Prophetessa, literally serving him as his spiritualized *soror mystica* anima, familiar to the tradition of alchemy as a working alchemist's "sister" accomplice and assistant in the Opus. This internal Maria, or Miriam, gave supraordinate mention for him what was the basis for his entire approach to psychology and alchemy in her documented homily that was especially precious to the New Jung as proto-alchemist: "One becomes two, two becomes three and out of the third comes the one as the fourth." Maria of Alexandria was thus the "new Woman" as Jung's *anima Juive* akin to the Gnostic Sophia (wisdom lady) as endopsychic "goddess" or what Parmenides enjoyed as the consultant he called *Aletheia* ("the unconcealed" as Truth).

On the other hand, the mystic Maria, like her Host had two personalities. Matching Jung's No.1 extraverted personality, she is represented as Salome. Livia Bitton-Jackson amplifies further and where Salome is "In search of an ideal, feminine Kingdom, she journeys later to the Russia of Catherine the Great, and the England of Victoria. Ever frustrated in her attempts to better the lot of her kind, she again finds Isaac who finally believes that their love is ripe for marriage. Salome realizes in wedded bliss that all her drive for power had been nothing but frustrated love. She even condescends to conceive and give birth to a child whom she names Homuncula, "little man, " and Ms Bitton-Jackson strangely concludes, "And so Salome, as all women should, falls into line," but goes on to note: "The Wandering Jewess as champion of women's liberation had been presented in a serious vein in a *fin-de-seicle* drama: *Ahasvera* (1895) by Victor Hardung."[51]

In that case, the extraverted adventures of Salome, like Jung's, come to a close except with the disappointment that militant Feminism has failed, indicating that unlike Jung "The Woman's" unconscious introversion is barred to further development. The parallel here is instructional insofar as Salome fails and must surrender whereas in Jung's case and his newfound interest in Alchemy, Salome is transfigured in the image of the Maria qua Sophia image as La Bel Juive. Accordingly, Salome is not defunct for Jung but establishes his unconscious parallel in process of what is going on in collective society and the world. Jung, now as *Homo Novalis* coincides with the New World Age of Acquarius and what I have characterized as "Animus Rising" representing a gynotropic culture event. That is the climax and telos of traditional feminine suffrage and feminism and which equally accommodates Jung's re-found introversion through the conversion of Jung's anima figures, first as Salome and then as Maria and both of whom are Jewesses and which does indeed cast Jung in his new inner journey as *Ewige Jude* but who will re-encounter Jesus only at the End of Days. Notably, the anima figures involved share in the nature of La Bella Juive not only her madona-like quality but the seductress as well, indicating that the animus at large is of a Faustian nature

Preceding further along the lines of Jung's destiny for his No. Two personality the Faustian animus that marked his No. 1 personality would till be in place supporting any erotomania and concomitant narcissistic obsession for career, fame and fortune. In his transformation, however, such residual elements of his Faustian No. 1 personality are mitigated it will be necessary to keep in mind Jung's interest, with some help from Carl Kerenyi, the Feminine Mystery religion and its mythos dedicated to the transformation of the feminine nature and how it is dyadically composed of two figures in one: mother and virgin daughter. Persephone, the virgin daughter, however, is fated to become the consort of Hades and thus the Queen of Death. And since Death (Hades) and Satan or the Devil are one of a kind, the figure of Faust lingers, especially as a psychopomp who finds the fair sex his inferior and where the feminine nature fares the worst as the Faustian exploitation of the woman and her limitation to the amorphous state of *Gefuhl Ist Alles* ("Feeling is everything"). "Feeling" is doubly used to on one hand designate woman as nothing but feeling and to the preclusion of "masculine" thinking by which to explain away Gretchen's belief in God, the better to leave the thinking to proper men represented by both Jung's No. One personality and Faust and their association with intellectual perpiscuity represented by Goethe. The same was true for Jung No.1, in both theory and praxis, with Dr. Freud and his pioneer "scientific" colleagues of Psychoanalysis. " Feeling is everything," however, as the ground for Goethe's poetics and understanding it as a surrogate for religion but abbreviated simply as "Nature" and the soon to become psychological state of a talking uterus otherwise later clinically abbreviated as hysteria. It served to limit the feminine estate to the paradigm of feeling as a form of unconsciousness. That is also echoed by Faust when asked by the pious Gretchen, "Do you believe in God" and by which the meaning of religion and the question of God, or poetry in Goethe's case, may be dismissed as adequate only to the pre-conditioned feminine feeling. However, it is also the source of Goethe's poetic intuition and its anima embodiment regardless there was no room for "Feeling" in the Kantian purview subscribed to by Goethe. Equated as such by the Germanic Man of Mind and thinking is its appraisal of both feeling and the feminine estate as in equivalence to unconsciousness. In similar manner, Jung's No. One personality would be reaffirmed as the elevation of masculine thinking and its privilege to exploit young ladies by seduction during an analytical transference. That, indeed was both the Faustian approach as well as the Arabic reason for being and its subsequent invading of a fast Christianizing Iberia during the early part of the first millennium. Pure and simple, the conflict with Christians amounted to a continued purging and diminishing of the feminine nature that stood in contrast to an alarming rise of the populist endorsement of the Virgin Mary, however it was merely tolerated in Papist theological doctrine. It was on the other hand, forcefully retained in the Mariological cults of Catholic women. The Christian doctrine of the Assumption of the Virgin Mother was early on in theological place but not admitted as Papal Bull until 1950. By no means would the pragmatic hands of the Arabic empirical and scientific magic of alchemy be able to tolerate so ludicrous a lingering notion of a Virgin Mother. Both The Islam and the Germanic Reformed Christianity, purging of such an image was coincidental to what was to become the case for the resistance to feminine "animus rising" especially when in mythogenic parity with the wandering Jewess and her climax as Sophia, represented by Maria of Alexandria.

The German Reformation diminish of the feminine estate was, however, outmatched by its colleague at arms, the Islamic Ottoman military might, and with its purging through the persecution of Christians in its conquered and occupied places, such as Albania, Macedonia and Constantanople were the feminist animus rising had origins in Thrace, Greece, Alexandria, The Balkans and the Mediterranean rim of North Africa from Syria to Morocco.

Little Sister

It was clear to Jung that the Germanic and Faustian relation to the underground phallic animus was far more intimate for him in personal terms than what is revealed in either the Feminine Greek Mysteries or the Romanesque and Latinate tradition of southern Europe. No. 1 thus made his choice, as did Goethe: "My mother, the whore, Who has murdered me--My father the rogue, Who has eaten me--My little sister alone. Picked up every bone, In a cool place she put them away; into a fair bird I now have grown; fly away, fly away!" (From Goethe's Faust).

The "little sister," of course, is also indicated as Cinderella or Little Lucinda, the last spark to survive the night and rekindle the hearth in the morning. Little sister thus prevails as another metaphor for potential and predicated as "virgin" or as Plato saw it as a substrate womb he called receptacle (xwpa), "as without previous impress" and that which is yet to come into being. In otherwords potential and the virgin were one of a kind. For Aristotle it was his prima materia as ousia (essence) without form and nihilio but, as such a pure and unconditional potential. In all cases and from a psychological standpoint, it is the anima as virgin and without previous impress by the animus. That would be the totally unawakened feminine nature. Its function likens it to that of Persphone Parthenos and in turn the virgin's need to comport with the Devil, in that case as the Lord Hades of Death taking the pure potential personified as his consort and Queen of Death. The marriage of Death with the virgin potential, however, is an anomaly except both the virgin as a state of nihilio, qua the unus mundus is precisely that absolute place of vacancy that must sooner or later explode, like apieron, and cast its enantia into the world as an active enantiadromia and active play of the complexio oppositorum by The One as Being gave way to ontos and the plurality of beings who had presence only because their consciousness was in potentia and be-coming. Jung's obsesional traffic with as if virginal young mistresses now began in new measure as the event of the Greek case, where the mythogenic venue begins with the realm of the maternal unconscious and its personification of a mother goddess and her virgin daughter was eventually abstracted as a concept of generation. In Jung's Germanic or Faustian case, by contrast, the mythologem begins with Faust's plunge into Goethe's "Realm of the Mothers" and by which the unconscious is understood more as a found object than as the given substantive of mythogenic representation. In the Faustian case, the Feminine nature is suppressed if not denigrated because limited and confined to a realm where it may no more than represent *gefuhl ist alles*, unconsciously promoted accordingly from the masculine standpoint that *denken ist prima*. In that case "feeling" would suffer the missionary position with the Germanic masculine "thinking" on top. Reflected, as such was Goethe's own two personalities polarized as his philosophical "thinking man's" affinity for Kant if not for *denken*, as such, and his "Feeling Is All" poetic genius that he attributed to Mother "Nature," but carried on the back of his Gertrude or Magarete. This immediately conditioned the ambivalence from the standpoint of the man-of-mind ego as a psychological rather than mythogenic paradigm and the more "natural," as Goethe would say, feeling man as the creative poet. But, it also demonstrated the ego's traffic with a brazenly devilish principle whose urge it was to incubus-like make itself available to all the women in the world and in history. Yet, aside from such prolific and supraordinate pro-masculine erotic *trieb*, it had equal assignment as Death and it is modus of destruction.

It would appear that Jung was in imitation of Goethe's personality ambivalence except for his dream as a youngster of the underworld phallic beast. Was this simply his psychistic premonition of the invasion by the Germanic blonde beast or an archetypal transgression quite independent of personal or historical commonality insofar as an archetypal ur-bild does not as a cathexis come into appearance except as an image or drive. It mysteriously arrives in the maternal unconscious as an underground phallic beast in the dream life of a little boy. If only acausally meaningful as a peculiar expression of synchronicity, precluded would be the possibility that this was not the little boy's "dream" but a projection of the maternal animus. In a mature male it would be, on the other hand, a psychoid event by which the bios of erotic necessity were at one with an endopsychic content. However, this would preclude the causalistic continuity of such a maternal projection by a woman ruled by the maternal unconscious.

The Teutonic Destiny

The Germanic Romanticist approach thus differs on two counts (1): the ego relation in empathic identification with the archetypal image of death as an object reality: (2). The notice of this image (as Mephistopheles) and its intended destiny to incarnate as a living principle of Evil on earth and of this world. It is thus stood in competition with the God on earth as He is in Heaven as well as the classical mythogenic realities of a given maternal unconscious evolved in classical Greco/Roman antiquity. Marked as such, is a distinction between the Germanic and the evolved cultures of Europe. It expressed a mood that was common to Schiller, Goethe and Nietzsche. Jung draws the conclusion accordingly, indicated as Faust's identification with Mephistopheles and, second hand, Jung's identification with Faust. In effect, this granted him "an increased feeling of inner security" if only that it provided for him a paradigm in method for connecting to the maternal unconscious and the chthonian underworld of Death. However, it does this most catastrophically in his immediately post-Freud psychotic episode of *Confrontation With the Unconscious that* commenced his attempt at integration of the personality and a process of psychological individuation. It would include the integration of his No. 2 personality and its neotenous little boy, the as puer eaternus. That would be the primordial ur-kinder as "Virgin" and as such, with the potential of the entire universe pre-dispositonally embodied as the Nihilio State of the unus mundus and its invisible immanence of potential. Nevertheless, this is what my Illyerian ancestor, Aristotle, was saying all the time: that "nothing" is the pleroma of the pure prima materia potential whose ousia or essence was comparable to the unus mundus that so impressed Jung in his big Mysterium Book. Or put more drastically as the "nothing and "zero" where there is no Being, if only the privation of Being but a pleroma filled with nothing but a pure and unconditioned potential, a mere ousia or essence that reverts back to the Receptacle (*xwpa*) of Plato as substrate womb that is Literally without previous impress or virgin. This in turn recapitulates Anaximander's apieron, or boundless that is "empty" except for it potential of entia or opposites that are "winnowed out" (apocrisis) to commence genesis. In all cases the virgin womb as biologic metaphor is invested in paradox insuring, as such that there is no misunderstanding that the metaphor is not either a rock hard object or in reference to the uterus but as a conceptual construct of the eidos. The especially Hellenic mode of thinking was, however, compromised when it arrived North via St. Thomas Acquinus, Paracelsus and Gehard Dorn that reduced the pristine thinking mode of Greek philosophers to a crass materialism of the alchemy imported from Alexandria. In either case the prima materia was reified as the Islamic stone, ka'aba or the Lapis (stone) or the Germanic hyper-mystical embrace of the material object which as an inscrutably closed womb trapped the Mercurious or what I otherwise refer to as "the Hermetic function" or endopsychic intuition. When finally freed it emerges as the fierce and destructive Wotonic wind raging in the Black Forest and destroying all in its path.

In the pre-Socratic conceptual integration there was something apparently lacking as a positive mythogenic resolution in Teutonic culture: Urtha, the forbidden underworld to which Balder the solar god descended was never to rise again as a new dawn. Continuity was maintained only as Ragnarok and the *Gotterdammerung* twilight of the gods, as it were, The End which endlessly repeated itself, end upon end, death upon death and represented iconographically as concentric circles whereas the Hellenic eidos was better iconographed as a spiral, a circling point that never repeated itself but rose up as ever expanding. In the Teutonic case, the ever-recurring new being was thus in direct causal relation to destruction. It is thus a coincidence of natures that Jung's two personalities follow in kind to the ambivalence of the duplex Goethe as philosopher/scientist and natural poet.

The catalyst for this is served by the "other woman, the "as if" virgin, the "little sister" and, of course, Little Lucinda (Cinderella) and all of whom combine in the masculine psyche as the desired mistress to invaginate as sublimated image of a daughter or younger sister and by which a de-facto incestuous relation is involved. This was also the case with Goethe and his philandering by which Jung claimed him as his ancestor. In either case such indiscretions (if only because spoken of) must lead from storm to stress and the final trieb as a personal twilight of the gods: or, psychologically, the coming down from an inflation and the breaking of a transference identification.

Precluding such resolution, the catastrophic implication of Ragnarok as a Teutonic destiny was less benignly modified by Nietzsche in his notion of the "eternal return." Return of what but Death and destruction! Jung, however, recognized the Teutonic Ragnarok as comparable to the modern destiny: He notes in his book, The Undiscovered Self: "A mood of universal destruction and renewal has set its mark for our age. This mood makes itself felt everywhere, politically, socially and philosophically. We are living in what the Greeks called the kairos - The Right Moment - for a metamorphosis of the gods, of the fundamental principles and symbols... So much is at stake and so much depends on the psychological constitution of the modern human."[52] On the other hand this is not a singular and unique historicistic event but "but every day of my (our) life." Now, in the year 2012 this is also dreadfully apparent and it is not simply a sign of the times but all times in or out of historical measure, e.g., the nuclear threat between the USA and the USSR mitigated because of their mutual possesion of the "God Bomb" now about to become pluralistically and polytheonically available, e.g., of the moment Iran in its shade as Aryan about to possess a nuclear weapon, ostensibly to exterminate the Jews once an for all time, who contaminate the pure Aryan blood of once Germany and the Ottoman Empire. Only then will it be fully deployed by the amateurs of monotheism and the "God bomb's" fulfillment as the End of Days when Ewige Jude, the Wandering Jew meets up again with the second coming of Jesus.

This projected reality is, however, no longer Germanic but "universal" and held closer to the Faustian climax and closure of a mythogenic Greek cosmology and its extension as Christianity. Yet, at the dissolution of the Christian mythos the universal destruction lies ahead and as if it did not depend "...on the psychological constitution of the modern human." It must instead assume itself as trans-mythogenic and pointing to the underworld as an object reality and its divine regulators subject to recurrent annihilation. It is frightfully comparable to the world course of the Third Reich and its climax in satanic abominations where the chthonian beast incarnate of intense and compelling rhetoric met its death in an underground "cave" (bunker) in besieged Berlin. But, it was also to be the fate of Jung's No. One personality as indicated in his recall of his traumatic "confrontation with the unconscious" psychosis. Thus, it stands today and no less as the voices of the dead and we who are about to experience our mortality.

Would this assume that Jung's No. One personality was object rather than subject related, indeed, a material piece of prophecy and by which his swift rise in career as a psychiatrist and psychoanalyst would perform as a substitute and replacement for his No. Two personality and its potential introverted interest in religion, spirituality and the Self. In that case, however, it need not have been as an animus rising as in the Greco-Latinate mythologies and then in the Christian culture evolution but the animus brooding in its underworld cave and like an earthquake in the making waiting for a crack or tectonic shift in the maternal unconscious to free itself. Rather than as a transcendental paradigm as in the case of Dante's descent to *L'inferno* in his Divine Comedy, or the three day sojourn of Christ in Hell before his Resurrection, the Faustian ego does not controvert the Devil but handily negotiates a deal with it just as God and Satan make a bet concerning the faith of Job.

It is thus a contradiction that Jung has problematically questioned the probity of God in his *Answer to Job* yet felt at home with Faust's pact with Mephistopheles. The cabal was not so much a descending into Hell and the *ignis ghennis* of Sheol, but in fact expressing a need to *redeem it on earth as it is in Hell!* In this manner, Evil and Death are subsequently entered as the "shadow" objects of (psychological) reality. Jung thus achieves, allowing both Death and Evil as ontological realities, in both the existential and phenomenological sense, i.e., as mundane *dasein* actualities or being in time and space. But, only the barbarity of Attila the Hun or Hitler and his Third Reich would satisfy such actualities and in the horrific paradigm of Caesar savaging Gaul, or however War and conquest may be explained away as the *privatio* of Peace On Earth and nothing more but a steresis following the phenomenon of enatiadromia where it is perfectly natural for something to roll over into its complement and served with an "Amen!" for the complexio oppositorum!.

Jung does this, however, according to the Germanic and Faustian mythogenic format and in doing so by forcing the archetypal parallel between it and Greek myth. It also reflects the Germanic approach to alchemy.

Drawing from Jung's interpretation of the German Spirit as the geni in a bottle fairy-tale: "It is worth noting that the German fairy-tale calls the spirit confined in the bottle by the name of the pagan god, Mercurious, who was considered identical to the German national god, Woton." Here Jung has assimilated Woton to Hermes just as Nietzsche assimilated Woton to Dionysius. He continues: "The mention of Mercurious stamps the fairy-tale as an alchemical folk legend, closely related on one hand to the allegorical used in teaching alchemy, and on the other to the well-known group of folktales that cluster around the motif of the 'spellbound spirit.' Our fairy-tale thus interprets the evil spirit as a pagan god under the influence of Christianity to descend into the dark underworld and be morally disqualified."[53]

Animus as Phallus Rising.

However, in the case of Jung's underground phallus dream, quite the opposite occurs and the Faustian beast emerges rather than descends. Such would be the case for the new epoch of the negative *Animus Rising* and by which a force of evil assumes priority in the collective psyche and thus duly expressed in the world. Apparently Jung had need to force the identity of the evil spirit to a pagan Greek god perhaps to forget that Woton is in his own Germanic keep, just as Nietzsche masked Woton as if he were the pagan dying and reborn god, Dionysius. But there is no rebirth for Balder, the Teutonic solar god and alter ego of Woton who, like the sun, sets in the West and never to rise again in the maternal East. Woton fares as badly in his *Sturm und Drang* cycle, the endlessly recurring twilight of gods and men. The demise of the Third Reich has now reborn itself as a global *veltgeist*. In the now unpopular Christian case, Death qua Hell is no longer intended to be conclusively overcome and hidden in its Bottomless Pit. In the Faustian approach, a pact is made with the invisible or irreprsentable Lord of Death as if it were, as an animus, the master in the maternal unconscious. In this way Jung and the current pagan revival is able to requalify a principle of evil as in equivalence rather than negation to both that of the Good and to God and where a principle of Evil is not simply defined as the absence of The Good or God (as with the theological doctrine of the *privatio boni*) but very much alive and well in the here and now: Death qua Evil allowed substantive presence by simply bargaining and negotiating with it as did God with Satan in the Biblical story of Job or, later, the old man Faust's bargaining with the devil for a taste of absolute (archetypal) ur-knowledge. Jung notes:

> The naive assumption that the creator of the world is a conscious being must be regarded as a disastrous prejudice which later gave rise to the most incredible dislocation of logic. For example, the nonsensical doctrine of the privatio boni would never have been necessary had one not had to assume in advance that it is impossible for the consciousness of a good God to produce evil deeds. Divine unconsciousness and lack of reflection, on the other hand, enable us to form a conception of God that puts his actions beyond moral judgement and allows no conflict to arise between goodness and beastliness.[54]

This is a provocative view insofar as it must further be asked "Who or what created Death" that prevails as the greatest Evil qua absolute evil? The privatio boni would thus have to infer that death is the absence or privation of life indicating that death is nihilo. This would assign death to Jung's appreciation of the unus mundus in its compare to the First Day of Creation as void. The privatio boni would apply in that case. But if, as Jung holds, such privation is "nonsense" simply because Evil (qua death) is, as a bonafide opposite, and as substantial as The Good and Life, it would equally hold that Death is substantial and no mere privation of Life.

This steresis in turn would contradict the unus mundus as void and nihil more so that Jung suggests it is the final unity achieved after life has passed. Dr. Maria von Franz paraphrases Jung; "In the unus mundus there was no disharmony, things were separate and at the same time united. Dorn says that the state of the unus mundus only takes place after death; in other words, it is a not a psychological event by which man becomes one with everything existing. Concretely the unus mundus manifests, as Jung pointed out, in the synchronistic phenomena. While we normally live in a dual world of 'outer' and 'inner' events, in a synchronistic event this duality no longer exists; outer events behave as if they were a part of our psyche, 'so that everything is contained in the same wholeness.'" Dr. von Franz fails to point out that the psyche like all and anything else would have no presence in the void state of the unus mundus "where duality no longer exists."

The unus mundus and the state of Death are, however, thereby rendered as a state of *Lethe* and total oblivion and which, of course, is a standard Atheist and materialist view. Nevertheless, it also equivocates as the First Day of Creation! In either case Death as the privation of life is not something in itself, i.e., ontologically substantial as a *topos*. The latter would be the desired conclusion:Death as something in oppositional equivalence to life. More provocative, however, is the inference that the unus mundus take some meaning as the pure and unconditional potential of the Aristotelian *prima materia.* In this manner, a conflict of opposites would be as simulated as simply a thinking man's logic of dialectical reasoning, e.g., Jung's alchemical attempt at reconciliation of the opposites in the unus mundus when, according to the defined nature of the unus mundus, entia would also be without presence. The logic here is inconclusive but which was not the case for Anaximander's apieron (the Boundless) which has a close relation to Dorn's unus mundus except not to consider only enantia are indwelled (as an immanence) in apieron. When "winnowed out" (apocrisis) the entia in conflict with one another endow the idea or elements object reality with necessity of the complexio oppositorum. In the Dornian and then Jungian approach, the unus mundus is taken as an end for the assimilation of the dead. No wonder hears the dead in voice crying out to him what else but Ja accuse!

Such an end or bonding with The One of eternity excludes, however, the *Woman* whether as mistress whose animus captures Jung's No. One persona, or her identity as virgin daughter of the mother, the immanence of virginity that a woman carries with herself to the grave. In either case the animus is Little Sister's genius, or animus genie, and is indistinguishable from the shadow side of Jung's No. One personality and his childhood phallic dream-beast rising in the underground chamber of the Mother's empty womb and virtual unus mundus.

Apparently the phallic animus persisted as no more than an unconscious libidinal dynamism for Jung and as if resisting "rising up" in consciousness. In the alchemical parallel the Lapis embodied Mercurious could be freed only through the intense alchemical opus and which precluded any sort of negotiation when it came to the *aurum nostrum* of the philosopher rather than the *aurum vulgi* of the alchemist "Quacker." The Quacker was their other word for the purely materialist alchemist and was a way of expressing discomfort with the Arabic alchemical materialism and its quest for the *aurum vulgi*. In addition, of course Jung's No. One extraverted personality is strictly adhered to what is psychoanalytic quackery so long as his No. Two introverted personality remained unconscious and inferior.

The Wotonic Bargain

There is, accordingly, no comparison between Woton and the Mercurious or Dionysus whom Jung also draws in to his suspected understanding of the underground phallus. Woton makes negotiated bargains, as in the case of Faust, when he exchanges an eye with the chthonian Mimir for the *ur-knowledge*. The surrendered "eye," I would suggest, is also represented by Baldur, the Germanic solar god who sets and never to rise again until the event of the Third Reich enacting at last "in the world" Heidegger's dasein. On the way, Nietzsche must announce "God is Dead" but which apparently assigns to the Christian God the fate of the Germanic solar god, Baldur. *Phos qua Phallus* remains in the underworld of darkness in the manner of Jung's awesome underground dream phallus. Controvert, as such, would be the Christian Resurrection and the rising up of God as the new dawn (Miriam) of the East (Easter) and the continuous renewal of Little sister and her virgin potential. Indeed, God is Dead means god qua Balder is never to rise again for Germany and now for the entire globe and its present day epidemic of Christophobia supported by Iran as Aryan determination to exterminate both Jew and Christian for polluting the purity of a hypermasculine culture.

That would be the final and never to be recycled twilight of the gods, the trans-historical climax and closure of the Teutonic *veltgeist* or *animus mundi*. In the "new world" Germany now must take a passive and mythless place in the world with its Scandic cousins because the Teutonic mythos has finally died once and for all for them and migrated to join a global pandemic as the Islamic Jihad. Such was not the case for the alchemical Mercurious whose rising up (and out) implied a telos for transformation not inconsistent with Aristotle's *entelecheia* by which the pure potential of his prima materia would resolve itself as morphe or forms in appearance.

Evidently, Aristotle's potentia served as Jung's "Unus Mundus" that in fact embodied Plato's apriori "archetypal intelligibles" or predispositions to forms in appearance as archetypal ideas as ides and the eidos. This, of course, sets the precedent for Jung's theory of archetypes and its empirical use in psychological praxis. Since, however, he never wagered with his baby dream image, his obsession for a non-existent empiric denied proper room for a psychological transcendental epistemic manifold. Or put in Platonic terms, the empirical as the antithesis to hyperousia and Plato's immovable Good, or if you will God. Hence, the best that may be said for Dorn's and Jung's unus mundus is that it stands solitary as the Platonic Good or summum bonum

Unlike Jung's forebear, Goethe, he could no more than leave behind a Kantian perspective by which *gefuhl ist nicht alles* yet cling to Kant's stupendous *denken* by which "thinking is all" as was the case for Jung's No. One personality. In other words, even in a psychological perspective, the Cartesian *cogito, ergo sum*, sets the rule, i.e., "I think therefore I AM and nevermind gefuhl is alles, better left to Goethe's Gertrude and the ladies' approach to religious feeling.

The Alchemical Intrusion

In the Germanic case, however, the Faustian ambiance was also preconditioned by the arrival in Medieval Spain of Arabic Alchemy, spiced with second-hand Aristotelian Macedonian concepts and dedicated to a primitive reification of Greek philosophical ideas in the material object. Aristotle's highly abstract concept of materia prima was subsequently embedded and rendered static in stone and had literally to be chemically retrieved from its entrapment in matter. Aristotle's *ousia*, however, was neither lost or entrapped insofar as it represented his process of Entelechy by which potentia was placed in a process of becoming to arrive as morphe or forms in appearance. The process involved was a principle of work (*qua opus*) called *energeia* and as the in fact a role literally taken up by the alchemist as less a spiritually hypothetical opus but a hands on and get them dirty in empirical process. In the alchemical case morphe was transliterated as matter so that it served to embalm the *materia prima*. Apparently the Arabic approach ran the process of entelecheia backwards and taking its ens as the beginning of the process. Starting with matter, however, has some psychological sense to it if "matter" is at all in equivalence to Mater or Mother. Its subsequent interpretation as *massa confusa* and the *nigredo* became symbolic references to what Jung came to understand as the maternal unconscious in its undifferentiated state. In the later Muslim case the stone at Mecca was literally the maternal egg that fell from heaven to become an immovable mother as the black stone of the ka'aba, perhaps as a literal phobic relation to the maternal unconscious and, in turn, the feminine gender itself. Hence, it had to be located outside the Mosque and place of worship.

A global conflict thus ensued insofar as the feminine nature also prevailed in the evolved Alexandrian presence of Christianity and its image of the two-in-one Virgin qua Mother. Nevertheless, the primitive haptic necessity of the Arabic approach to Greek ideas was well suited to the pre-philosophical German resistance to Christianization. Created, at that early age, was the peculiar affinity of Germany for Islam and the German alliance with the Turkish Ottoman Empire finalized as their defeat during WWI. This amounted simultaneously to sympathy for Christophobia and hatred of the Jews. As much was equally expressed in the early Muslim invasions of Spain and by which it could not only resist the Christian doctrine but subvert it with the alchemical materialist goal of chemically transforming base metals into gold.

It thus served to reinforce the medieval urge to reify a mythogenic content or an abstract concept into thing and material object. This, of course, was further replicated as the Reformation and its total rejection of mythogenic generation but leaving behind in its shadow the Arabic magical spageric praxis and imagination that, in its inability to grasp the prima materia of Aristotle's essence of matter, except reduce it to its own origins and the worship of a sacred rock that fell from the heavens. Thus, the essence of matter was literally reduced statically to stone by which the Lapis was objectively located in origin as from out of this world.

Curiously enough, this would relink Jung's embrace of alchemy with his later speculations about the object actuality of UFO's as a from out of this world transgressive intrusion, no less as the big headed bug-a-boos emerging from the unus mundus as strange encounters of another kind. It also corresponded to the material objectification of the prima materia as the unus mundus, indeed a one world out of this world serving as psychological paradigm for the Self but more subliminally as a modern day intellectualized hereafter to deposit one's dead body and soul!

The Arabic blend of materialism and magicism, *materia qua seclorum*, also provided a displacement of abstract and transcendental thinking such as it was known in classical antiquity. On the way empirical science as we know it was born. It also left the question open for Jung of whether the lapis from outer space was in fact simply the evidence in collective consciousness of a psychologically transgressive archetype or, in fact, an extra-terrestrial objective event. Following his idea of synchronicity and the psychoid archetype, it was no doubt both. Jung's, from out of this world, notions are certainly timely for the collective anticipation of either a catastrophic invasion by destructive heavenly aliens or their presence as a panacea for all the ills of the world insofar as they replicate the coming of the Paraclete at the *End of Days*. Extinguished, however, on the way to reification of a concept or a mythogenic property, was the original Greek ontological approach to being and necessity. However, even worse, equally purged was the Greek mythos and its Feminine Eleusinian Mysteries and the supraordinate Virgin feminine represented by Persephone, later integrated as the Mother of God as both mother and virgin. In this way a contra-feminine ideology took hold and was reflected in the various Christian Brotherhoods and climaxed in the *Aurora Consurgens* of St. Thomas where the prima materia was likened to odious uterine filth as *Aurum saeculum redivivum,* as it were, the feminine prima materia as no more than issued from a fouled pudenda. Indeed, the essence of matter, along with the Femina creatura was taken as filthy and unclean and in need for purging and transformation into the well cooked and sanitized masculine *Femina sanctum* or *candida* of the alchemical soul image. It was, accordingly, complemented by the obsessive world need for the *aurum vulgi*, the transmuted metal of solar yellow now reduced to the negrido of fossil fuel.

The Pejorative Feminine

The feminine as soul, psyche or anima then stood polarized to the Gold of the market place and later as Mercantilism. It was then that the persecution of women began in earnest and continued into modern times and further activated in the Sharia code of modern militant Islam. That would bring the negation of the feminine in head on collision with the embattled remnant of Christianization and its Virgin Mother in the West and more especially in final conflict with the current rising American gynocracy where the feminine ideal follows a masculine (qua the animus) mode of being or a new race of "men without penises," The animus proto masculine woman. It would represent the essence and ens for what I have specified as Animus Rising. It was as if the underground dream phallus had already broken out: *der phallus ist lose*, along with the *Hunt ist lose, der katz ist in der Keller* and the *Burgomeister ist kerplatz*, or so I heard when ashore in occupied Germany and dared ask a fair Fraulein, *Vas ist los?*

At War's end and always at the end of a war, the archaic animus rises up and is at large serving the arrival of a gynocratic era and its conclusion in a global regression to the maternal unconscious. Christianized Spain early on had already responded to the anti feminine revival with its Inquisition of both Arabs and Jews from Africa and their alchemical philosophers who migrated further East on the continent. The Arabic prima materia as archetype of the maternal unconscious was better left hardened as the *Ka'aba*, safely isolated in the courtyard at Mecca, precluded as such for presence in the sacred precinct of the Mosque. What was suppressed in either case was the concept of "virgin" as the "little sister" radix of potential and no less wrought in Aristotle's idea of the prima materia that by the Christian epoch was extrapolated to "Virgin Mother" as the archetypal representation of potential unconsciously invested in the figure of a Virgin. Notably the concept of potentia and the virgin nature overlap as materia prima as was the case with the Platonic *xwpa*, or receptacle womb without previous impress, i.e., virgin.

Aristotle's materia prima signified pure potential and later found its iconic investment in the figure of a virgin, no less a virgin mother. The contradiction was implied for a patristic ruled society.

The Arabic Harem, following the Old Testament practice assimilated such distinctions by identifying the feminine person as a plurality fit for only one function; the production of a son. Hence, a plurality of Virgins was promised but only in the after-life and which, of course, precluded a singular and all pervading Virgin Mother. The Christian feminine extended the Feminine Mystery Religion of Greece that was centered in the ambivalence of Mother Demeter and her virgin daughter, Persephone, as one person in two parts that, astoundingly enough, requalified the woman as a whole person and an ontological singularity, something reserved only for men who enjoyed the dyadic feminine as mother/wife and the inner anima. However, this would also indicate the proximity of the anima (as Persephone) to the underground Hades as representing a phallic animus shared by both mother and daughter.

It was a first indication of an animus called into play as the necessary agency for the individuation of the woman. In a patristic society, such a process was barred even to men except abstracted as Aristotle's concept of entelechy. In the Feminine Mystery religion by contrast, it was ritually concretized as the emotional and supraordinate experience of the initiate (mystae) and at once establishing it as a knowable psychological event. In this sense, the psychological experience was barred to men who were mentally limited to thinking and whose higher mode of being was limited to philosophy.

Nevertheless, many men from over the known ancient world entered themselves as mystae in the Mystery religion. It is thus notable that men saw fit to overcome the psychic and the mental, or otherwise said, the *Eros qua Logos* contention as the opposites per se barred to reconciliation and unity. What Aristotle neglected in his entelechal formula was the underground or unconscious maleness promoting the Demeter/Kore (mother/virgin) reconciliation of the opposites: and that is to say, the gender polarity of enantia.

Such maleness took form as Hades, then Hermes and finally Eros and all of who had a distinct phallic attribute if not, as in the case of both Hades and Hermes, were represented as a phallus. Such an image was barred and banned in Patristic society as the devil itself and endowed as the principle of Evil.

It is thus a momentous realization indeed, when the image of an underground or "hellish" phallus appears to a three old boy, reportedly as a dream, as was the case for C.G. Jung. I would say it was as momentous as the event of the Assumption insofar as the phallus remained trapped and hidden in the underground of the maternal unconscious much like the Hermetic Mercurious remained embodied as a prisoner of the Stone, or Lapis. The Animus Rising, as such had a vast collective significance whose full consequence has remained dormant except as the animus rising cult of men without penises that tempts modern women out of whatever agoraphobic tendencies they may suffer. The embodied Mercurious animus was equally in fact an extension of the phallic Hermes trapped in the Mother lode which, in and of itself, was the obdurate maternal unconscious that would never easily let go of its progeny of potential and which soon enough became limited as the role of the (in) House-wife.

The mother, however, from her original incarnation as virgin was another story. Through the virgin nature, representing no less the Aristotelian pure potential offered some form of egress from the Mother-stone. It was thus featured as the primary anima of the masculine psyche by which his potential in the world could be realized in a process of individuation. Nevertheless, of even vaster significance is it for the feminine nature. What is most notable here is that the virgin nature has a special imperative relation to the Hadean underground phallus.

As an anima figure for the male the virgin not only represented the Little Sister potential but also demanded some in fact actual phallic attention from the male. Such attention cannot be extended to either

95

mother or wife who are often one figure for a married man. From the individual male standpoint this as if virgin potential was projected as a young woman known as the extra marital other woman or "mistress," the anima and its *ur-gestalt* animus and its potential. On the other hand, it may be also be referred to as the Spirit of the anima or animus of the anima. It then performs as the animus at large or animus mundi as zeitgeist and regulator of collective consciousness or "Kultur" per se.

Animus of the Anima.

Considering that Jung nearly wrecked his marriage for his necessity to indulge in young as if virgin ladies, it is clear that the process of reconciling virgin and mother as a singular female person was near impossible. In the balance stood his No. One and No. Two personalities as opposites in conflict that would take a lifetime to realize in coniunctio and hieros gamos as an unus mundus and which would reduce the work for selfhood as pure nothing or perhaps eclipsed in some nirvana that reaches for the state of lethe (oblivion) before body and soul are parted by the Lord Hades. On the other hand, any inversion in the matter resulted in the given bios and gender identity at odds with its psychic complement to the effect of psyche reaching for the complement of the given bios to the effect of a transgenderization by which Homo qua Homo, the same for the same has the greater appeal than heteron or the Other. Along these lines, it may be said, that the process of abstraction seeks The Other whereas its complement as empathy enjoys the same for the same.

After separation from the standard psychoanalytic ideology Jung more distinctly drew the line between the Germanic urge to abstraction and that of the Latinate expression of empathy. In his Psychological Types, he observes how Wilhelm Worringer's *Abstraction and Empathy* marked the difference between Germanic introversion, and its envy of the empathic Latinate extraverted comfort in the realm of a sensual and hands on relation to the object. The southern feeling into extraversion, of course, evolved from a tradition emerging from the classical polytheonic anthropomorphic identification of mortals with the immortal gods. Both trends were in the measure of directional priorities, the latter beginning with the maternal unconscious as ground and the need to "rise up" from it and the former as the necessity to Alchemically enter the maternal unconscious and free the all powerful Mercurious as agent Hermeticum. Hermes Trismigustus (thrice powerful) thus came to represent the underworld Trinity of Hades as Death, phallus and Animus. This would assume that the Faustian predilection originally enjoyed a primitive extraversion quite in the measure of Jung's No. One "Arabic" personality and its need to redeem the No. Two where good and evil were not simply one the exclusion of the other but both opposite and equivalent. First, the realm of the mothers and its feeling is all would have to be declared as a product of Nature as in the case of Goethe and his *Urphainomenen* ("primordial event"). The *denken ist prima* was finally climaxed by Nietzsche and his option for The Dionysian music of the mothers and abandonment of Apolline illumination and a concept of beauty, implying the transformation of the philosopher (as Nietzsche himself) into a poet of the Sublime. Indeed, this was to ultimate as the Rock 'N Roll of the alchemical endopsychic static noise: of the "rolling stone" Lapis and the ever-transforming *trieb* of the *Mercurious ist los* in the world as the spirit gone wild for a historical destiny, e.g., the Wotonic rise of the Third Reich.

Here the Hermetic nature exposed itself in duplicity as the Mephisthophelean image of manic excess and death, more however, when reinterpreted as the demonic Woton as a raging killer and icon of the blonde Beast of the pure Aryan or Iranian race. As much is not far removed from the peculiar Faustian obsession enjoyed by Jung in his interpretation of alchemy as the problematic nature of opposites according to Gehard Dorn the German Alchemist. In this analog was concealed Jung's wrestling with his two personalities as a conflict of opposites closer to home and in the backyard of his soul: what was beyond words and thoughts materialized as the substance of his No. One Personality and its given shadow as the monstrous underground phallic dream image. He is thus obliged to note in the Forward of his Mysterium book:

> "The obvious analogy, in the psychic sphere, to this prob-
> lem of opposites is the dissociation of the personality
> brought about by the conflict of incompatible tendencies,
> resulting as a rule from an inharmonious disposition."

This in fact reflects not only a self-diagnosis by which "The repression of one of the opposites leads only to a prolongation and extension of the conflict, but a cataclysmic world catastrophe, the silence of the unus mundus overcome by an unthinkable explosion such as, from my subjectivist standpoint, when my ship exploded due to a defeated German need for revenge. In other words, psychosis from individual to collective event is an irremdial collision of the phylogenetic and the ontogenetic Zoë from Bios. Where then is the therapist who confronts the opposites with one another and aims at uniting them permanently. The quick solution to this unity is realized as the unus mundus but which has apparently dissociated itself from its Zero precedent and awakened the prospect of death as a totalistic annihilation. The irreconcilability of the two opposing personalities would thus be overcome by the alchemical process of "permanently uniting them" as an unus mundus serving the materia prima as *Massa Confusa* and original chaos. Jung thus predicates the above statement as: "The initial state, named the chaos, was not given from the start but had to be sought for as the prima materia. And just as the beginning of the work was not self-evident, so to an even greater degree was its end." Such was not the case in Egypt during 342 BC with the founding of Alexandria and views of Aristotle promulgated. The unity of the unus mundus thus remains entirely ineffective as Jung further implies: "There are countless speculations on the nature of the end-state, all of them reflected in its designations. The commonest are the ideas of its permanence (*prolongation*) of life, immortality, incorruptibility), its androgyny, its spirituality and corporeality, its human qualities and resemblance to man (homunculus), and its divinity." In short, the unus mundus may be used as an analog for life after death and a given ontology of a hereafter which is hostile to life or any other substance in being or by which the unus mundus as pure being serves to annihilate ontos and the plurality of beings, (such as ourselves).

The goal of such grandiose cosmic pathologism would thus be limited to uniting the elements of the opposites in one form but which as the unus mundus is alarmingly synonymous enough with death as a "place" beyond time and space and all that is given to being withdrawn. Aside from that, human qualities merely have a "resemblance" to divinity and which remains as such a mere transcendental persona or cosmetic reality and, as such, an accidental appearance of form in being. This is, of course, not the case when what is on earth is as is in Heaven but dialectically reformed as on earth as it is in Hell. So begins the epoch of existential phenomenology now climaxed as post-modern relativity where all human values are reduced to idiosyncratic affectations. The transhistorical culture process, however, alarmingly coincides with its service to accelerate freeing womankind from its prison of the womb and by which an animus rises to the effect of achieving a gynocratic political hegemony, first in the

USA and then globally. At hand would be both the physical and psychic unigender or, more accurately, the epigenetic and political abolishment of gender per se and the humanoid as no more than the Platonic androgyny unsplit and waiting for the renewed event of duplexity to defuse enantia or the opposites upon which is based the evolution of species to the greater effect of adaptation and survival.

The Fusion of Opposites

As much is reflected in President Obama's popular "great change" directed not simply to the position of the 99% class of underprivileged Americans but all in kind in both America and The World. He arrives, of course, as the American paradigm of categorically directed or "correct" thinking, an animus mouthpiece for a *gehful ist alles* hysteroid public of men without penises and women without vaginas and the arrival of demos as supraordinate androgyny. Transformation then becomes a case of fusing one opposite with another so that both lose distinction. This is, of course, only a generalized indictment of any public leader from dictators permanently encosed as such to duly elected presidents elected for a limited venue. It then becomes clear that the political persona must be a feigned or borrowed one suitable for general and public appeal or what amounts to loss of soul and degenderizing of anima and animus. It makes, accordingly, less transparent to the public the self-persona of the politician as essentially narcissistic, self-centered and self serving, who is, as it were, in effect entrapped by his public constituency and which has the effect of inducing a duplex persona as both self-centered and *pro bono* by which the Leader maintains power. Consequently, the politician is necessarily "all head" but no "body" of his own but his/her public one. It is thus a matter of intensity of the expressed will to power from Head to Body that determines who or what, the Head or the Body, is the greater victim of auto-entrapment.

The duplexity involved, however, is merely an application of the common two personality syndrome tautologically bent back on itself that characterizes masculine personality affectations brought on by the male heterosexual confrontation with the animus. Jung notes, "The man, or the masculine ego-consciousness, is then contrasted with an animus, the masculine figure in a woman's unconscious, who compels her either to over value him or to protest against him."[55] This, of course, is contributory to the masculine two-personality syndrome. It would be as if what Jung highlights as the complexio oppositorum is built into masculinity. In hermeneutic interpretation this may, however, be taken to extremes that are self-contradictory with regard to the inateness of hermaphroditism. "In this connection" Jung notes, "it should not be forgotten that in antiquity certain influences, evidently deriving from the Gnostic doctrine of the hermaphroditic Primordial Man, penetrated into Christianity and gave rise to the view that Adam had been created an androgyny...Christianity is neither male nor female, it is male-female in the sense that the male paired with the female in Jesus' soul. The tension and polaristic strife of sex are resolved in an androgynous unity...The consequence of this is a special emphasis on bisexuality and then on the peculiar identity of the Church with Christ, which is based also on the doctrine of the *corpus mysticum*. This certainly forestalls the marriage of the Lamb at the end of time, for the androgyne 'has everything it needs' and is already is a *complexio oppositorum*."[56] In other words, it is a question of arriving (being) before leaving (becoming) and precluding what is the dynamic of Aristotle's entelechaeia, the principle of work or energeia. However intrinsic this violation may be it is essentially a pro-masculine projection of the complexio oppositorum as something native to the masculine, per se.

Nevertheless, even worse, it represents a fusion rather than unity of opposites by which the differentia of male qua female are totally fudged or rendered undifferentiated. However, it may be upheld as a mystical state of mind it succeeds only in banishing the Body from the Head. The formula must thus paraphrase, "I aint got no body" because the narcissistic head has first option on reality. It may also be said that where the Body, and bios per se are concerned, their substance is as deeply repressed as the soul or anima, the inner or unconscious nature of the masculine psychology. Hence the negative view of the Binarius as representing the female *creatura* as a slut, the twoness of the Devil. More likely in demonstration here is hardly "bisexuality" but *Homo qua Homo*, a passive (latent) or active homosexuality, the head denying the given bodily gender organs and their function. The affectation is especially human and typical of its withershins. In either case what is in total denial is the physical and biological natures of gender which must, accordingly, be suppressed along with the anima or soul and by which *homo*, or the same, overcomes, *hetero* the other.

Archetypal Entrapment

What follows in this regard is what I must morbidly refer to as archetypal entrapment: or living out an unmediated apriori pattern in the life experience, in this case the animus as collective *Geist* in its most archaic circumstance exposing itself as a given persona identity for either the person or the collective at large and which may be one and the same for each. The "mother-phallus" objectified as persona immediately raises the question of the more active role played by Jung's No. One personality as in equal fact a man talented with directed thinking: e.g., Jung's early work, e.g. his *Psychology of the Unconscious* that marked his break with Freud and later (1920), his Psychological Types whose construction is an example of directed thinking at its best. It demonstrated object seeking and his extraverted attitude that highly motivated his need for a perfected career. It also included the extraverted thinker as especially addicted to the Faustian habit of seducing young ladies as if to suck dry the virgin potential they seemed to embody. That is to say, the persona identified with the Devil in its erotic predisposition as well as its relation to Death, Hades, Hell and destruction. Indicated, as such, is the invasive great big phallus rising up in Jung's early dream as if to later Alchemically materialize as Jung himself in his affective No. One personality and its extraverted demeanor. Prophetically enough, it is this animus that is now at large in the World as the *Zeitgeist* driving *Spiritus* or *Animus Mundus,* behind the gynocratic amplification on its way to global hegemony in a "Nanny State" that is no longer ideologically predisposed as "socialistic." "Marxist," or "Fascist" but simply and structurally an imbred form of mono-capitalism turned in on itself and where only the great leader is availed individuation, or it's facsimile, thereof. In that case, a talented directed thinker serves as puppet persona for the gynocratic animus. However, this new matricentrific male apparently stands as complement to the less recent patricetric regulated extraverted "thinking type" male that includes a transgressive sexuality and its sex object. It was this form of induced narcissism and which is the forced imperative of a Leader, that the more libidinous young Jung may have been taken for granted by Freud when he accepted him as more useful as an extraordinary man of the world who appeared most qualified to serve the Emperor as the "crown prince" of his Psychoanalytic Empire. In that case the narcissism is shared, and which amounts to a strictly persona love affair, e.g. when Jung served as Freud's ambassadorial guide in their trips to America and the attempt to transmit the sexual revolution to the

New World. Their effort, however did not bear fruit until after WWI and the out of hand "Roaring Twenties and the proliferation of illegal booze where "The Body" overwhelmed "The Head" whether dancing the "Black Bottom" or awash in bathtub or speakeasy booze.

Hardly in sight for Jung before that time was his sequestered infantile No. 2 personality centered by the well concealed "rising up" animus figure whose destiny was to compromise his formidable directed thinking and its extraverted object seeking propriety. The breaking through of the primordial phallic animus was, however, initially achieved by the instigation *in actu* of the "other woman," or as Jung later called it, the anima as unconscious contra-sexual image for the masculine psychology. In effect, In the collective response to such "roaring" in America, the underground phallus arrived as the Empire State Building, the greatest and tallest building in the world but which is soon enough compromised by a hyperinstinctual giant, archaic and appropriately called "King Kong" and with the collective anima in hand screaming her bloody head off. The great beast personified by absorption the narcissism of Great Leaders, such as, at the time, Pres. F.D. Roosevelt under whom Prohibition was repealed and which was followed by a de facto form of socialism, or collective matricentricity, called the "New Deal." All of this, mind you, took place within the brief span of a few years and all of which and at the same time was lent paradigm and parody by the Four Marx Brothers in the their hilarious but forebodingly prophetic movie, Duck Soup.

All of the above occurred a few years both sides of 1933 during the Great Depression. Some levity was perhaps necessary to offset the Manifest Destiny of the USA as redesigned by the President, something provided by the Marx Brother's and their cinematic parody of the Nanny State called "Fredonia." *Duck Soup*, was an hilarious early Marx brothers tour d'force cinema satire of what appears as the coming and going of the Socialist state before it arrived about the same time as the either the Wotonically mad Third Reich or the "Happy Days Are Here Again," New Deal. Since the film was presented in 1933, it was no doubt made the year before. It thus pre-empted the fuller nature of German National Socialism instituted by Mr. Hitler & co., also in 1933. It was as if the Marx brothers were mocking something that had not quite yet come into being but was about to in at the time, continue intact after WWII and using the necessity of a war to solve the economic failures of the Nanny State, past Korea, Vietnam and Iraq wars and finally come to fruition and openly declared the State is the master of the people's fate openly and without shame proposed by Pres. Obama. Consistently in the opening scene of Duck Soup bailout is proposed for the failing utopian nation of Freedonia followed by internal dissension, revolution and finally resolved in a great war, Marx Brothers style. H.G. Wells is thus comedically outdone in his *Things To Come* and which was about to come again following the final solution to the Great Depression in a Great War some eight years later. In Duck Soup's grand finale, Groucho, of course, is elected, as Pres. Roosevelt's or now, Pres. Obama's counterpart, although more prudently, and with greater unwillingness to serve as interlocutor for the destiny of Freedonia. In this way the 1933 film comedy dissipated any reservations the public may have had for the implementation of the New Deal by FDR's left hand man, Harry Hopkins, who no doubt had better in mind for a brand new *United Socialist States of America* (USSR). The film also included the role of Harry Hopkins hiring Chico and Harpo as secret spies to infiltrate Freedonia. But what was also compounded in such acausal coincidences of a third kind were such unruly Depression Day events and its New Deal was the eponym of *Marx* brothers with Karl Marx and that of the name *Roosevelt* which literally means *Red Land*. If one has the wit for it that is less than dim, words may entertain themselves in this way as I have presented "word synchronicites" in a previous work. Such coincidences did not ruffle my duck feathers except give me pause for a good laugh that was often painful in the world expression of acausal meaningful coincidences and which is to say are events as means but without ens..

Jung Soup

It was the animus of this anima that was "rising up" as the Depression Day King Kong with screaming lady in hand perched on the greatest monumental phallus ever risen and which was no less in parallel to the gigantic and rising-up underground phallus of Jung's latent No. Two personality boyhood dream. In this instance, however, the anima is in the image of his psychoanalytic patient and then mistress, Sabina Speilrein, who in her intimate relation to Jung inspired his concept of the "other woman" or anima. However, it equally expressed the animus in the world at large and more especially in the booze restricted U.S. of A. where bootleg whiskey and beer and sexual promiscuity marked the epoch of the "Roaring Twenties. Is eventually mitigates through a federally induced state of collective depression the psychology of which is masked in notions of financial and economic meltdown.

In this case, the rising gynocracy must effect an extensive cleaning of the slate of all residual masculine priority. Even after the demise of the various patristic national Socialisms after WWII, Jung found further need in 1957 to notice in his *Undiscovered Self* the power of the state as in fact a source of de-individuation: "Instead of the concrete individual, you have the names of organizations and, as the highest point, the abstract idea of the state as the principle of political reality. The moral responsibility of the individual is inevitably replaced by the policy of the state (*raison d' etat*) ...Such one-sidedness is always compensated psychologically by unconscious subversive tendencies. Slavery and rebellion are inseparable correlates. Hence, a rivalry for power and exaggerated mistrust pervade the entire organism from top to bottom. Furthermore, in order to compensate for its chaotic formlessness, a mass always produces a leader who infallibly becomes the victim of his own inflated ego-consciousness, as numerous examples in history show."

The possibility of totalitarian contingency to the Zeitgeist, postured as the archaic invasive phallic nature of the rising up animus has, of course, been related to world events as the soaring missile in flight to its target. On the other hand, the modern behavior further exemplifying Jung's philandering is something familiar to the collective form of male behavior that has lingered as a compulsive necessity. It expressed the masculine necessary, but secret tradition, for enjoying both a wife and a mistress; something affecting men of the apparently highest moral and ethical caliber who were celebrities in the public life. It was as if it were an archetypal given that they were destined to become unconsciously personified as the animus of their own anima: that is to say, the "maleness" of each their own "other woman" and unconscious soul image as anima that would amount to their duplexity of unconsciousness, i.e., doubly unconscious of themselves.

The resemblance here is to the narcissistic "Great Dictator" whose inflation is politically self-serving. The result is an item of unconsciousness that is not too easily resolved, if at all, and integrated in the masculine psychology and life experience. Whether it should or should not be something more than lip service in the moral pretense of such men and their escorts (of either sex), is disputable. It is, however, accompanied with an inflation of the personality and subsequent will to power leading to an autocratic leader. Aside from such political ramifications the unconscious lust for the "other woman" certainly did not spare Jung: The Other that is, to either mother or wife. As the heteron or hetaera anima, it represented the "unknown woman" embodying for the male his unrealized potential and, as such, in the order of the Faustian entree to the maternal unconscious, or however a negotiation may be carried on with a Mephistophelean contender.

The political consequence may then be personified as a leader who infallibly "becomes the victim of his own inflated ego-consciousness," driven by the unknown woman anima. However, will this still be in place for the new gynocratic society of matricentrific men who are at home in the realm of mothers, mother-in-laws and animus driven wives? Indeed, will maleness no longer be identified with the psychological animus but the animus as pure spirit, a seminal conveyor of potential whose paradigm is no longer the phallus but the Paraclete as Savior of the World. Even as it now stands the idea of the Spiritus Sanctum as the seminal discharge that generates a son without disturbing a virgin womb is unthinkable if not a blasphemous reduction of the Divine to biological metaphor. Nevertheless, as much will be sustained as the new gynocratic spiritual correctness of the animus inflated woman and her modern collective of "men without penises" constituting the base level of contemporary feminism.

Same sex love and marriage equally represents liaison with an unknown potential in an offbeat lover. More descriptively, the other woman or man not only is as if a daughter or a son to the maternal aspect of the unconscious but represented by an as if virtual virgin nature, i.e., the as if "straight" heterosexual. The male is more often drawn to his other woman from an erotic standpoint and hardly aware of her psychogenic ground as the unextended "virgin" nature of potential. A homosexual person may equally target a "straight" person as their virgin in potentia. The virgin nature was, however, long ago understood by Plato as a "receptacle" (*xwpa*) or womb-space without previous impression and further abstracted by Aristotle as the potential of the prima materia.

It was at this junction that the Germanic introversion and the Latinate extraversion combined to make up the European and then American collective soul. The "other woman" came to rule the masculine psychology, if not the Euro/American destiny with the animus of the anima ruling the mass global culture. What this in fact eventuated was the "split" of the

Western personality into two halves, consciousness and the unconscious and which in turn effectuated the ubiquitous phenomenon of the presence of two personalities in one person: the manic inflated personality alternating with the depressed personality that appeared from a clinical standpoint the safer condition and thus brought to bear. In the past cigarette smoking served this purpose until it was banned and replaced by smoking "grass" as the collective pacifier. I have no doubt, accordingly, that WWII would have been lost to the Allies if cigarettes were banned and the quick fix of "lighting up" were not available to momentarily ease anxiety.

The Ethical Anomaly

Taking this archetypal entrapment of the male to heart in my senior years I at once saw myself "all my life!" living this out but even worse, equally demonstrated by men who represented my highest ideal, in this case C.G. Jung. Coming to terms with my own erotic compulsions produced a trauma by which I was not what I thought I was. Here an ontological rather than psychological question was raised. I wondered whether the philandering behavior of Jung with his extra-marital mistresses was no less the same compulsion celebrated by U.S. Presidents Jack Kennedy with the voluptuous Marilyn Monroe or Bill Clinton with his hapless interne servicing him orally from beneath his presidential desk in the Oval Office. Certainly I could not understand myself as given to such ludicrous and obsessive indulgence for the simple reason that I had no celebrity life and thus spared the inflation contingent to it and by which the male was publicly wagged by his tail. The inflation was actualized as the male giving in to philandering or "wandering" in overt if not emotional necessity for betrayal of his wife and their marriage vows. The need to indulge the "Other Woman" as the source for his unexplored potential was to overcome a psychostasis in his identification with mother/wife. A "Little sister" was required to share her potential: in bed, of course, to service the psychostatic male. More recently, such was the near identical case of Governor Spitzer of New York State who decided to resign after public disclosure of his rather expensive adventure with a most attractive young lady of a brothel. In most cases, the wife "stood by her man," almost as if she was in cabal with the clandestine hetaera lady. The wife appeared to serve as an enduring and patient mother figure in the relation of her husband to the "other woman" who was non-other that a virtual family endured Little sister or daughter.

The syndrome is especially noticeable in politicians running for office and no matter nominalistically counted as a deficiency of character, hardly unexpected. It was thus publicly acceptable as a virtual fantasy by women of themselves as Little sisters and by men who could not do without them. In either case it was an urge to separate from the mother who in turn sought "eternal beauty" through the mystery process of re-virginization by which the mother herself redeemed her own virgin potential as was the case in the feminine mystery transformation process. Indeed, the mistress, as projected anima of the male, became the daughter of the mother\wife. It thus appeared as if a cabal by mothers and daughters, wives and mistresses, to in fact abort the male fantasy of achieving his full potential.

This was also the case with President F.D. Roosevelt and his secretary mistress, Lucy Mercer. Such ubiquitous triangles, whether anecdotally fancied or *in actu*, may have just as well found cause for any man confronted when the "honeymoon is over" and thus moved by a "seven year itch." And which has less to do with a marital circumstance but a midlife crisis of the soul confounding metaphor and paradox as a spiritual confrontation with the idea of death. In that case, death as a metaphor becomes a paradox of what is unknowable.

Because a wife more often served as mother to both the man and, if any, their children, it became urgent for the husband "to be born again" through the agency of a younger woman whose uterine estate was fantasized as somehow virgin in contrast to that of both mother and wife. She was at best "virgin" for him whether her uterine traffic matched that of the Holland tunnel. Whether she was a prostitute or an actual virgin was all beside the point insofar as she appeared as an unknown quantity of the materia prima or, otherwise, as the psychistic untouched uterine plenum of potential. At last, the Aristotelian prima materia had become psychologically grounded in human bondage relationships insofar as it was qualified as in the modus of pure and undifferentiated being represented by the unus mundus. However that may have been tolerable for the Arab invaders of Iberia, a St. Thomas reconditioned by the object-fixations of alchemy and its subsequent reduction of the feminine estate as a filthy, corrupted bottomless pit fit only for traffic with an alarming giant phallic animus such as baby Jung allegedly dreamed. Was this a moral issue compromised by a psychogenic if not archetypal necessity? Did it place the psyche and its invasive *archetypus mundus* as the greatest of evils (for the male) as necessarily pathologized and in turn over-riding such ontological questions of both "who am I" and "what am I" if indeed I Am at all true blue and morally authentic? Was ontological correctness and its standard safety surrendered to this compulsion for the as if unlimited endopsychic potential of the Other Woman? Finally: was an actual sexual connection the necessity of such relationships that may have just as well served as the bait by which to get the male unconsciously hooked on the possibility of potential and renewal?

So irrational is this compulsion that we find Martin Heidegger, as the rector of Freiburg University during the early days of the German Third Reich, take on one of his young Jewish students, Hannah Arendt, as extra-marital "little sister" mistress. But, Jewish little sister! His wife's extreme addiction to the new German National Socialism and its anti-Semitism apparently was not strong enough for her husband to surrender his young La bella Juive girl friend.

In Jung's case this seven year itch, right on schedule at 35 years old, involved an irresistible need to explore his Number Two personality, in effect his latent introversion hardly at rest in its unconscious maternal state. For Jung No. One it was regarded as no more than an intellectual abstraction, the extraverted affectation regulating his career and ambitions as a strong "thinker" in the early Psychoanalytic movement. Yet, Jung's personality No. 1 was unable to resist temptation by the as if unlimited feminine as womb of potential.

My own peculiar fascination for this phenomenal necessity overlooked that every male whether from a higher or lower conscious state of development required a mistress for him to become more than he was. This included just about every President of the U.S. to every male marked in self-importance, and/or hubris and the Western necessity of an inflated personality. Whatever their station, such inflation was the earmark of the Euro/American male, if not a need to transcend the "common man". It may be noticed that this male developmental necessity was omitted for those cultures where the male enjoyed a harem and who accordingly, never got past the primary male ego. For the developmental male, however, the inflation of the personality was prerequisite and in direct relation to the unconscious quest for potential. For the American woman it is passed on as the animus in kind and root to the gynocratic culture trend enforcing itself as a (female) race of men without penises.

Recapitulated as such was the Faustian necessity of the collective male actualized as the first love and matrimonial obligation that was violated more so because wife had been combined as mother, mother-in-law and grandma but to the exclusion of little sister or daughter who, as a virgin, represented an unconscious potential for an apotheosis of the personality. In short, unterman must be overcome and attained as uberman resulting in a superman complex of unlimited potential. What lurked as the unconscious complement to the superman was the ontological anxiety of mortal man at Death's door.

Perhaps I had neglected to notice this in my own case, because only after my marriage had come to an end, did I take up with a most obliging young lady fifteen years my junior and with an Ivy League education. She thus did very well as my bed-partner and researcher, editor or my de facto virgin womb of potential reflecting my anima state as a daughter figure or, if I was alchemistically inclined my soror mystica. Only technically was I not a philandering "cheater" but which opened wide the question of the need by an older man for a young "other woman" as both bed partner and lady of assistance not only in his work but the very quality of such work for the very reason that he has projected into her younger self, all that is seemingly virgin and a source of (his own) potential in Faustian terms if not his own approach to the question of death.

Jung, was also in fact, replicating in his affairs, the tradition of magicians whose work companions and assistant women served equally an erotic purpose, e.g., known, for the alchemist as the *soror mystica*. Such women, as with Simon Magus, who bought his Helen from a brothel, remained inferior. So long as the "sister" as consort was predicated as "mystic" the implied inferiority was softened. This follows in the tradition of seers and wise men and their Faustian need for a Helen of Troy.

At this time I was fascinated by a sketch, I had drawn of a nude old man with a long beard and an erection in hot pursuit of a nude young lady. At 38 years old, I was hardly an old man except as in a relation of an older man to a younger woman. It was becoming clear to me that mother and wife did not fit the bill for what Jung called the "anima." The anima was indeed designed in temptation, Lilith herself, the woman as irresistible because an unknown quantity in terms of the male's potentia in lethe, concealed, that is, from his normative prime personality and functioning subliminally. Such was, as the archetypal image of the anima in potentia, cast as a daughter or a younger sister and, accordingly, barred to conscious amplification by the taboo of incest. The sister, qua daughter as if virgin image was more easily in unconscious sublimation to avoid the incest taboo, or the possibility of child abuse.

Whatever the statistical frequency of such abuse remained obscure because it prevailed as either a secret family affair or openly expressed pathologically as a criminal indulgence and a matter for the police. Short of that, the person of the other woman as "mistress lover" was remote and which offset an unconscious incestuous necessity. Even more anomalous was the circumstance personified by the "virginity" of the other woman because it need not have been charged with virtue but equally well served in the posture of a harlot or prostitute.

The "other" was in fact a euphemism for "inner" and, as such, beyond the propriety of an "outer" reality. The bait in all cases was the as if erotic necessity to visit the womb of such a figure and where the penis served as an invaginating, object-seeking ego. Unconsciously presupposed, of course, was the virgin predisposition of young women of the girlish kind and by which "virgin" implied for the male a pure and unrealized agency of potential. Yet, in all cases a mother was included, not only as a "mother-in-law" but one that was outside of all law: the maternal unconscious itself. Its matricentrific necessities included the male (qua the animus) embodied and trapped and thus serving as a hermetic son. It was represented as phallus and serpent and later evolved as Hermes and the Mercurious. In this primordial archaic form, the maternal animus made itself known to baby Jung and shown rising from its underground entombment as if "back from the dead," in his Alexandrian soul.

Freeing this animus took form for Jung in his urgent need to evoke his No. Two personality and rise up his underground maternal phallus. Early on, in his 1919 publication *Psychology of the Unconscious* he equates this phallus with the rewards of a revealed introversion: "The snake represents the introverting libido. Through introversion, one is fertilized, inspired, regenerated and reborn from the God. In Hindu philosophy this idea of creative, intellectual activity has even cosmogonic significance." This "significance" is still the No. One personality thinking in hyper intellectual terms yet ominously aware that the place of transformation is really the maternal uterus: "Absorption in one's self (introversion) is an entrance into one's own womb, and at the same time a form of asceticism."

At the time he was barely aware that the via regis of the uterus was not that of the mother/wife kind but the sister/daughter image unconsciously sought in his various mistresses. Here we may take the maternal unconscious as the greatest unknown and, accordingly, as the matrix of the greatest potential quite in parallel to the concept of the materia prima as pure and undefined potential. On the other hand, its complement would lay dormant as the all and opposite to an idea of new being. In either case sister or daughter was unquestionably marked as "inner" or endopsychic realities of access to the underworld. Apparently, even as I composed my mother/daughter mystery I was barely convinced that mother was not separate from the psychistic virgin daughter and its fuller implication to what Jung included as the unraveling of his No. Two personality, such as he experienced it in his Confrontation with the Unconscious. That was, of course, after the fact of his transference indulgences with girlish Sabina and Toni.

More difficult is it to know when the male is more the animus than himself, or the female more anima than an actual woman. However that may be it is the animus that assumes the aggressive prerogative to assert what should be rather than what is. In either case, the personal reality is submerged and an archetypal reality takes over, manipulating its hosts to transpersonal ends. More often this evolves as a conflict having little to do with external circumstances or even personality differences but an internal developmental process suppressed and hence gone wrong: that is, as an autopoesis serving its own structural ends rather than that of it's host, the result of which may be understood as an "archetypal entrapment" for the wandering male.

Such was the case with the extremely talented, funny man comic, director, producer and actor, Woody Allen, who had an irresistible need to run off with his adopted daughter, to the utter chagrin of actress Mia Farrow, his wife. Woody took the necessity for a mistress beyond its more common demonstrations. As much, however, would not have rattled Jung and as if such entrapment of the male was not by his own volition but provoked by his anima personifying an unconscious dromena. Mr. Allen, however, went straight to the mark and chose a daughter much in the manner of Hades, Lord of Death, who ravished the virgin Persephone. From his professional standpoint Woody is devilishly creative, taking from his subjective standpoint what few cinema innovators would dare. For all his "nebishness" he deserves the Iron Cross for action in combat.

From this same standpoint, an unconscious factor bonds the wife and the mistress, or other woman, in a mother daughter relation. Only more recently did I notice that Jung's alleged mistress, the young Sabina, his first patient, was in effect a daughter image in relation to Jung's wife and mother of his three daughters. Jung found himself in phallic service to both as the now proverbial "big prick" animus erotically (and heroically) shared by both women. The actual erotic exchanges that took place were in turn determined by a deep unconscious psychism, in effect, a complex by which the three figures were knotted or what I otherwise refer to as "archetypal entrapment." Indeed, Jung the visionary genius of Depth Psychology was human after all! Was he in fact philanderous or more subject to the cryptic intensity of the transference where, indeed, the innocent virgin was also an unlearned but convincing seductress? Indeed, she was the personification of Persephone as the Queen of Death or consort of Hades, virtual Cleopatra and Mary Magdalene femme fatal no less better personified as Leonardo's Mona Lisa with her enigmatic smile: "Lover, beware, I am going to eat you alive and suck your spirit right out of you, animus mine."

All such virgins in feigned in innocence and were in deep transference with Jung and what amounted to either overt or secret (unconscious) love affairs compounded as their awe of the man. Jung, as such, thus performed as an animus that proved irresistible from a woman's unconscious standpoint. Was Jung aware that his underground "rising up" phallus was the animus of the once virgin Queen of Death? Would that account for his prolific need for very young ladies of only apparent innocence? Apparently, his persona provided an animus image of the male as a semi-divine figure by which transference and love were combined as a form of worship with no less than Philemon as its alter ego.. This, of course, was not so unusual in terms of love relationships not, at least, until after Freud's sexual revolution. Soon enough, such affairs were no longer autoerotic fantasies as the culture materialism of the flesh overcame all spiritual reserve. The actual erotic adventure, that included a Jeykel and Hyde vigor became more public and no longer confined as the Original Sin of the world parents in the Garden of Eden. The extra-marital excesses of public figures such as Presidents Jack Kennedy or Bill Clinton hardly ruffled the political feathers of a voting public collectively in transference with them.

In the more traditional sense, Hades as abode of Death became the standard Greco-Roman place reserved for non-material ghosts or shades. Even the Boundless (*apieron*) embodied only the opposites as a dynamic rather than material and in being elements. This would, of course, assign the complex of opposites to the ontological state of Death and, as such, to a tautological self-creation of opposites. It would amount to Death creating out of itself or in and by itself like a Kantian noumenon. The proposition would, indeed, violate the *privatio boni* and what was for centuries held *sui generis* by philosophers and theologians alike as an impropriety. Indeed, Jung's "little girl" patient, as Freud called Sabina, had dropped a hot potato in his lap. It later stimulated him to follow up Empedocles who went one step further than Anaximander: naming in kind, as in the Second Day of Creation, the coming into being of four elements that paired up as opposites: water/earth, air/fire. Jung, not to pass up a good opportunity, psychologically replicated this in his formulation of four fundamental psychological types: feeling/water, earth/sensation, air/thinking and fire/intuition.

Such a reduction of material elements to nominalized psychological types is achieved without the full entelechy accounting for the generation of material elements from potentia to telos. That would leave the type theory as purely analytical and as such tautologically predisposed and without substance. That is, however, also the problem with Freud's Psychoanalytical as well as Jung's Analytical Psychology insofar as the "objective reality" and *tertium quid* of a scientific approach is centered in the closed circle of mutual experience bonding analyst and analysand and by which they remain a self-predicating or tautological reality. On the other hand, maintaining a scientific perspective would substitute the psychological reality with an objective premise that would subordinate if not inhibit for both the doctor and patient the virtual "love affair" that takes place in the transference relation. More bashfully, the Freudian analyst prefers sitting out of sight by the patient in such intimate intercourse whereas the Jungian with bolder Gentile effrontery prefers a persona to persona engagement.

If nothing more, Jung's transference wrought love affair with the young but inspirational Sabina Speilrein provoked his interest in Art. His closeted Red Book contained renderings that were more appropriate to a Medieval time rather than either contemporary art or alchemical images. As an art form and yet quite inventive they could only be classified as primitive and hardly aesthetically welcome in the Modern Art venue. Strangely enough, Jung was an astounding designer rather than painter and by which his pre-thought images were rendered with great skill. He would have been otherwise an impressive graphic designer.

As if justifying his own closet art approach was Jung's cavalier treatment of Joyce and Picasso, who were more *a'la mode* as creative personalities at the time. It is thus surprising that his own art attempts along with his mystic poetry nevertheless found him evaluating both Joyce and Picasso from a purely psychiatric standpoint when he generously notes: "Hence I regard neither Picasso nor Joyce as psychotics, but count them among a large number of people whose habitues it is to react to a profound psychical disturbance not with an ordinary psycho-neurosis, but with a schizoid symptom-complex." This was expressed much after Sabina had come to Jung in a dream or vision announcing that he should give up the practice of psychology because he was in fact really an artist. Jung notes in his Memoirs: "When I was writing down these fantasies, I once asked myself, 'What are you really doing' Certainly this has nothing to do with science." He then fancied a voice that came to him "from a woman I recognized as the voice of a patient, a talented psychopath who had a strong transference to me. She had become a living figure in my mind." Indeed, Sabina had invented herself for Jung as what he later called the "anima." However, even as so late a time as his writing his Memoirs with Aniela Jaffee, his secretary, he attributed this as:.

> That is the way a woman's mind works. I said very em-
> phatically to this voice that my fantasies had nothing to
> do with art, and I had a great inner resistance. No voice
> came through, however, and I kept on writing. Then came
> the next assault and again the same assertion: 'That is art.'
> This time I caught her and said, 'No, it is not art! On the
> contrary, it is nature,' and prepared myself for an argu-
> ment. When nothing of the sort occurred, I reflected that
> the 'woman within me' did not have the speech centers
> I had. And so I suggested she use mine. She did so and
> came through with a long statement."[57]

Subsequently, Jung became the voice of her animus that apparently and conveniently did not have "speech centers" and which he provided, thus serving, as it were, as the animus of his anima. Was such also the case with his other analysand "lovers" ("talented psychopaths)?" The making of art and entertaining conceptual intuitions remained his blind spot if not more appropriate to his slumbering No. Two personality. Like Goethe, he considered art as given by "Nature." Apparently the making of art if not poetry and philosophy were far too psychopathically and irrationally (intuitively) inclined for his No. One personality and its "directed thinking." It was thus his tendency to suppress and transfer them over for study by a female colleague, e.g., such as Sabina Speilrein, then Toni Wolff and in the case of philosophy to Dr Maria-Louise von Franz and finally, Aniela Jaffee who was of major assistance in helping putting his Memoir together. What he was experiencing in all cases was what has since become known as the anima. The anima in this capacity has precedent as Parmenides' goddess. Martin Heidegger notes: "The thinker Parmenides tells of a goddess who greets him as he arrives at her home in the course of his travels. To the greeting, whose proper essence the goddess herself clarifies, she ads an announcement of the revelations she has in store for the thinker as he goes his way. Hence, everything the thinker says in the subsequent fragments of the 'didactic poems' is the word of this goddess. If, at the very beginning we pay heed to this and preserve it well and rigorously in our memory, from then on we shall take our direction from this insight, to be acknowledged gradually, that the dictum of the thinker speaks by bringing into language the words of this goddess. Who is this goddess? We anticipate the answer conveyed only by the 'didactic poem' as a whole. The goddess is the goddess 'truth.' truth-- itself-- is the goddess."[58]

The process of coming into being (be-coming) is in fact replicated in Martin Heidegger's notion of da-sein. Significantly enough, Heidegger also figures in an extra marital romance with one of his young female students (Hannah Arendt). The Mythogenic scenario is finally transcended in Jung's old age and the assertion of his more introverted No. Two personality, e.g., as his hyperousia affection for the unus mundus that he represents as the agency of pure potential to be realized as the analog to the Self. In this sense both of Jung's crypto-transference young patients were not only chosen for their *in potentia* (as if) virgin natures but for their quality to reify themselves as the *femme inspiratrix* aspect of his anima projected into actual women, provided as the "other woman" or Hetaera, hardly as phantom psychosis but with moist vaginal lips.

The alternate valence to this anima was, of course, the mother (Demeter) in the figure of Emma Jung, his wife. The original maternal projection of Jung as the primordial and hence ubiquitous phallic animus is thus virtually lived out and by which both extra-maritally indulged "daughters," Sabina Speilrein and Toni Wolff. They were for Jung anima auxiliaries to "Mother" Emma Jung and in a Demeter qua Persephone, Mother/Virgin Daughter relation to her. As if Emma did not have here own daughters to guide but her Hadean involved husband presented her with his cache of Faustian prizes, from Helen of Troy to Clymenestra, seductress to Sophia, the ur-wisdom sought for by Faust in his bargain with Mephistopheles.

The highly broadcast and so-called philandering by Jung with his mistresses (Sabina, Toni, etc) raises some suspicion that such affairs were exclusively carnal, There may also be some doubt about sexual penetration. The question was, did Jung suffer chronic erectile dysfunction in reaction to his intense fantasy life, something that set in after his marriage to Emma and fathering his children. His crypto-philandering crisis arrived not by way of Emma but his children (e.g., the poltergeist episode) and when he first retired to secretly cloister himself to do his Red Book.

Jung was in trauma at the time, not only because of his split with Papa Freud but a sort of gynophobia derived in an endopsychic shadow form of the feminine (anima) by which it possessed the persona and subverted the ego. Thus, obsessionally indwelled (passive introversion) sexual function would tend to fall back in repression and without compare to the intense, if not overwhelming fantasy life. Indeed, Jung was hardly a super-stud for the ladies and falls into the same category of Bubba Clinton, who truthfully "never had sex with that woman" if at all what went on with his young interne under the Oval Office desk may be called "sex.".

It may also be noted that Jung's hyper state of inflation engendered a form of self-delusion with regard not only to sexuality but his fantasy life insofar as he believed Philemon & co. were sprung from his psyche when in fact it may have been a case of cryptoamnesis that he forgot the details of his previous studies in Goethe (his alleged ancestor) and the figure of Faust. The recapitulation may have indeed been compensatory and where Faust was finally redemptively white-washed as the figure of Philemon who flies off into the wild blue yonder mitigating, as such, Jung's No. 1 personality guilt for his extraverted hiatus with Freud and then his "affair" with his first patient who Freud, perhaps sarcastically, alluded to as the (his) "Little girl."

Indeed, even the thought of incest and its taboo can turn a man inside out with hardly a clue that he serves as a walking, talking, pontificating animus for all "little girls" to come, from Sabina, Toni, von Franz, and finally A. Jaffee, not to mention an inner sojourn with Salome in his Red Book account where he described Philemon as being an old man with bull-like horns and kingfisher wings, who clutched a set of four (4) keys. The four was Jung's endopsychic trademark for commerce in the process of individuation.

For Jung, the quarternio was, however, best endorsed by the alchemist Jewess, Maria Prophetessa of Alexandria and largely based on the Gnostic tradition, But she may have just as well served as an utterly mythogenic anima for Jung insofar as she was an inspiratrix in the measure of the world as the path of Knowledge (Gnosis) now assigned to Philemon. In mission was the Faustian compulsion to awaken the spiritually dead or, more accurately. the walking dead, e.g., in Jung's *The Seven Sermons to the Dead written by Basilides in Alexandria, the City where the East toucheth the West.*

Jung observed that he later realized this archetypal blueprint and other fantasies resulting from his confrontation with the unconscious during the period 1912-1930 first documented in his Black Books, and then his secretly produced Red Book. Marie-Louise von Franz, Jung's most important disciple, noted that Philemon replaced the Jewish prophet Elijah in Jung's active fantasy as the embodiment of wisdom and was also identified with Metatron, the chief angel in the Judeo-Christian tradition, who in late antiquity, was also considered to have been incarnated in both Enoch and John the Baptist. More dramatically, however, he was often impersonated as the Eternal or Wandering Jew.

Von Franz went on to show how these figures, especially Elijah and John, were depicted as unusually hairy, a characteristic of Merlin of the Grail tradition. Merlin, it is also worthy of note, is reputed to have a Christian mother, a pure virginal woman, and the devil for a father. This has a distinct relationship to the Greek Eleusinian Mystery cult of Mother Demeter and her virgin daughter, Persephone, also known as the Kore and Parthenos. Coincided, accordingly, is the abduction of Persephone by Hades, also later known to Christians as the Devil, a substitute term for Death (Hades), personifying as such, Death as the greatest Evil known to mortals and along with its complement, sexuality and underground "rising up" phallus revealed in Jung's three year old baby dream. Hence, The greatest evil (Death) in its ambivalent form is represented by The Serpent and its phallic iconicity.

Ewige Jude

The mystery deepens here when The Lord of Death (as greatest Evil) chooses the virgin Persephone (as greatest agency of potential) to serve as his consort and Queen of Death. Here a concept of death and virginity overlap. Along with this, also neglected by Jung in his alleged fantasy account of Philemon qua Elijah is their relation to Salome who is linked to the Wandering Jew, also known as Ahasverus or Buttadaeus. In Jung's case, such climax was anticipated in his traumatic identification with Faust. It is, however, considering his rejection of Christianity, reconstructed in the early German legend of the *Ewige Jude*, the Wandering Jew who was cursed by Christ when he paused while carrying the weight of the cross and was taunted by who became known as the Wandering Jew.

As Christ was carrying his heavy cross from Pilate's hall and towards his place of crucifixion, Ahasverus, then in Pilate's service, mocked Jesus for walking so slowly. Christ, in turn, doomed him to tarry in this life until his (Christ's) return, that is, until the Second Coming, a period that would take 2000 years. What this deathless wanderer in time does, however, is fornicate, his way in Faustian fashion and, along with Salome, all the way to the end of time.

For Medieval Germans Ahasverus was linked to their pre-Christian but lingering god, Woton, also personified as a restless wanderer and, as such, represented the *leit motif* of the Nordic, Scandic and Teutonic people who are also reported present in the Egypt of Rhamses and known as the "Sea Peoples." For the Israeli of the time they were also known as the Philistines more often in conflict with the Israeli (e.g., qua David and Goliath) but eventually integrated with the Hebrew people. Palestine, for example is an eponym for Philistine and which is still problematic for modern Israel.

Only in the Second Day of Creation are parts named after their kind. Avoiding such distinction the unus mundus, for all Jung's pretense for empiricism and scientific method, is a metaphysic that serves to justify the epistemic priority of the unus mundus as an absolutely empty and vacuous pleroma whose only justification would have been Aristotle's notion of his prima materia as equally void by virtue of its necessity as the immance of the pure potential. But neither Jung or von Franz take full account of Aristotle even as Jung speaks of Alexandria "where the East meets the West," as if this was his purely fantasy notion when it was in fact the arrival of Aristotelian notions in Alexandria and their meeting up with those of the East and Persia. Such historical facts certainly mar the authenticity and originality of Jung's celebrated fantasy in his now publicly broadcast Red Book. It may have been, however, that Jung was dreaming aloud what was the historical event of Alexandria by which Alexander introduced Aristotle to Egypt. But even more grievous as the historical record goes, neither Alexander or Aristotle were "Greeks" and representing a Hellenic hegemony, but of ancient Albania then called Illyria. But what takes priority is the notion of Aristotle of the necessarily empty pleroma of pure potential that just happens to coincide with Dorn's notion of the unus mundus and his goal to bond for all eternity with the unus mundus or world as hyperousia.. Not so strange, therefore, that Jung would borrow the concept as paradigm for the psychological self and its realization during a psychological process of the integration of the personality. That would be reasonable enough except it would be understood in terms of Aristotle's enetelecheia and its process of coming into being. Then Jung lapses metaphysical rather than psychological when he proposes that synchronistic events (meaningful coincidences) are experiences of unus mundus in life and acts of creation in time. The acausal nature of synchronicity means that such experiences are not primarily causally determined but are orchestrated by the Self as unus mundus. In that case a God concept must be appropriated to accommodate the all seeing eye of the Self qua unus, and by way of conveniently enjoining the Self with what Jung posited as the *imago dei* or by his definition as no more than the psychological rather than metaphysical image of God. Again, the reduction to psychologism fuses a metaphysical proposition (synchronicity) with the *in actu* reality of psychology. The oxymoron is implicit But no matter insofar as the image of Philemon is called upon in a general Jungian view, to lend apotheosis to such formula because he eventually integrated spiritual meaning, along with a spirit of nature like the alchemical Anthroparion, who insists on making things real in the physical world. This is in reference to the homunculus or little man who is at home in the less than celestial unus of the winged Philemon. The question is, does *uberman* enjoy the divine position as if in the service of *unterman?*

Alexandria and the Dead

Curiously enough, the Anthroparian is cited as a goblin when in fact he is non other than the common man in the Anglo Saxon and American purview. Perhaps this goblin nature adds the crippled leg included in Jung's projection of Philemon. Indeed, if the leg represents an inferior relation to earth and ground, best thing to do is fly as the quickest means of escape from mortality. Would this indicate the figure of Philemon as totally detached from the mortal condition and hence more likely at home in the realm of Death, Hades, Satan & co? But, of course, why else would Jung call on the dead in his *Sermones ad Mortuous*, ostenasively located in Alexandria! Enter at once the realms of Macedonian Greeks such as Alexander and Aristotle and the daughter of that place, Cleopatra, and the Ptolemaic Egypt of about 300 bc that opens a realm of the dead that is part of a living history on its way to migrating to Iberia and then to the Medieval Germany favored by Jung. The Dead of Alexandria, however, has more to offer that would titillate Jung from the depth of his Hermetic being. Accordingly, the original Cleopatra must set the pace for those femme fatales to come, such as Mary Magdalene, the mistress of Jesus, all the way to Leonardo's Mona Lisa and all of whom are set in the archetypal forbearance of Persephone Parthenos who becomes the bride and consort of Hades, as it were the Queen of Death. In token of all such ladies of fate I must begin with a fuller account of the original Cleopatra who, like myself, was of Albanian (Epirote) ancestry and known as Cleopatra of Macedon: and not to be confused with Cleopatra Eurydice, the Macedonian wife of Philip II. Nevertheless, Cleopatra of Epirus, who was an Epirote-Macedonian (Albanian) princess and later queen regent of Epirus. The daughter of King Philip of Macedon and Olympias of Epirus, she was the only full sibling of Alexander the Great. Her other siblings include half sisters Thessalonike and Cynane, and half-brother Philip III of Macedon.

She grew up in the care of her mother in Pella, like a normal princess. In 338 BC, Cleopatra stayed in Pella with her father while her mother Olympias fled to exile in Epirus with her Molossian brother Alexander I of Epirus (Cleopatra's uncle), and Cleopatra's brother Alexander fled to Illyria. Soon Philip felt he had to ally himself to Alexander I by offering his daughter's hand in marriage. A large wedding between Cleopatra and her uncle Alexander of Epirus was held in 336 BC. It was at the celebration of her nuptials, which took place on a magnificent scale at Aegae in Macedon, that Philip II was murdered. Immediately after her father's murder, the two newlyweds went from Macedon back to Epirus. Not too soon after, the couple welcomed two children, Neoptolemus II of Epirus and Cadmeia. Leaving Pella did not mean leaving her family behind, as it is believed that Alexander and Cleopatra kept in close contact while he was on his conquest to the East. In 332 BC Alexander had sent booty home for both his mother and sister, as well as his close friends.

In 334 BC, Cleopatra's husband crossed the Adriatic Sea to the Italian peninsula to campaign against several Italic tribes, the Lucanians and Bruttii, on behalf of the Greek colony Taras, leaving her as regent of Epirus. She was involved as recipient and sender of official shipments of grain during a widespread shortage around 334 BC. According to an inscription from Cyrene, Libya she was the recipient of 50,000 'medimni' of grain, and shipped the surplus to Corinth. Alexander I conquered Heraclea, took Sipontum, and captured both Consentia and Terin, but was eventually killed in battle in 331 BC, leaving the young heir, Neoptolemus too young for the throne. Cleopatra thus ruled Eprius in the meantime. It was an Epirote custom that the woman of a family became head of household when her husband died and their son(s) were too young, unlike the rest of Greece. It was only fitting for the powerful queen to assume control. When her husband was killed, an embassy from Athens was dispatched to deliver condolences.

She was more surprisingly but seemingly acting as the religious head of state for the people of Molossia. Her name appears on a list of Theorodokoi ("welcomers of sacred ambassadors"), in the recently established Epirote alliance. Cleopatra was significantly the only female on the list. Her position as official welcomer would have allowed her to keep a finger on whatever was happening anywhere in Greece. Around 324 BC, Cleopatra went back to Macedon, while her mother, Olympias assumed control in Epirus, as relations between the Macedonian mother-queen and Antipater were quite strained. It was not long after that Alexander the Great died in 323 BC. After the death of her brother, she was sought in marriage by several of his generals, who thought to strengthen their influence with the Macedonians by a connection with the sister of Alexander the Great. Leonnatus is first mentioned as putting forward a claim to her hand, and he represented to Eumenes that he received a promise of marriage from her. After Leonnatus' death in 322 BC, Perdiccas next attempted to gain her in marriage. After his death, her hand was sought by Cassander, Lysimachus, and Antigonus. She refused, however, all these offers. She escaped to Sardis, where she was kept for years in a sort of honorable captivity by Antigonus.

An interesting event took place in Sardis. A frustrated Antipater publicly accused Cleopatra of being involved with Perdiccas in her half sister Cynane's death. Cleopatra would not submit so easily, however, and fought back. Eventually, Cleopatra acceded to a proposal from Ptolemy, but before her design could be realized, she was captured. After being brought back to Sardis, Cleopatra was assassinated in 308 BC, seemingly by order of Antigonus, who afterwards gave a beautiful funeral in her honor.[59]

All of the above may appear pertinent when it is considered that Shakespeare cast his *Twelfth Night* (or *As You Like It*) in Albania (ancient Epirote and Illyria) and Jung dedicated his mystic proem as "The Seven Sermons to the Dead written by Basilides in Alexandria, the city where the east toucheth the West." Moreover, of course, Alexandria was founded by Alexander the Great of Epirote and whose sister marked the beginning of an evolution of a certain kind of woman situated "where the East toucheth the West."

The Mystic Jewess

Act Two: enter the mystic Jewess and womb to Alchemy, Maria Prophetessa. Ah, would not Jung be united in a hierosgamous with this Jewess for her prognostic aphorism that was not only the alchemical formula but was to become the theoretic ground for all Jung's reckoning in his Analytical Psychology: One becomes two, two becomes three and out of the third comes the one as the fourth. The arrival of The One is, of course, the unus mundus later supraordinated by Gerhard Dorn as his chosen hereafter. For the German alchemist, and then Jung, not so curiously, a Jewess stands as marker in Jung's psychological perspective. However, here is an unmentionable cryptic love affair except for another femme inspiratrix in the figure of Jung's first patient, Sabina Speilrein. In her diary she notes: "Now pair No. 4 [meaning she and Jung, ed.]. That is the present masculine pair. The Christian in it my friend; he is a doctor, married. Other elements such as strong religious sense and the sense of calling, are things of which he possesses more than enough, for his father was a minister! At the time our poetry [their cryptic hyper transference love affair, ed.], he had two girls, and the potentiality for a boy within him, which my unconscious ferreted out at the appropriate time in prophetic dreams [no doubt to be sired by the doctor as her Messiah,ed.] He told me that he loved Jewish women that he wanted to love a dark Jewish girl. So in him, too, the urge to remain faithful to his religion and culture, as well as the drive to explore other possibilities through a new race, the drive to liberate himself from the paternal edicts through an unbelieving Jewess."[60]

Sabina encapsulates the then barely found Jung with a need for a Jewish lady. This was an astounding piece of foresight, something not uncommon for her if not an aspect of the Eternal Jewess as companion to *Ewige Jude*, the Wandering Jew. She takes on figure as Salome who appears in Jung's Red Book.

"The Wandering Jewess," notes Livia Bittton-Jackson, "is a most versatile myth. It has been adapted to many issues political, religious, social and it expresses contradictory attitudes toward Jews both good and evil. In this respect the Wandering Jewess is a unique atypical image: she combines the stereotyped figures of the Jewish male and female, the figure of the sinister, evil Jew and the sweet, kind Jewess. Even her most frequently used names, Herodias or Salome, imply feminine wiles, ambition and the power of seduction alongside virtues explicit in the narrative. Who is this wonder woman, this mysterious Jewess mother of mankind"[61]

Is it Salome, Mother Mary or Miriam, star of the sea, or simply the ur-bild of the archetypal Jewess who, as gripping Sabina when she laments: "must day and night dream: He told me that he loved Jewish women that he wanted to love." Here we find Jung cast as the wonder man half of the wonder woman Jewess and groomed for the role of *Ewige Jude* and translating past imprudent Faust and his alter-ego, Philemon, to the Jew of all Jews on his way to seeing it all through to the End of Days and the Second coming. Only then, in meeting with the refound Jesus, would he be granted the right to die.

Oedipous and Philemon

Curiously enough, the Anthroparian is cited as a goblin when in fact he is non other than *unterman*, the common man in the Anglo Saxon and American sense. Perhaps this goblin nature reminds of the crippled leg included in Jung's projection of Philemon or, otherwise Oedipous, which also means crippled foot or leg. Need it b e said that both Philemon and Oedipous are high fliers where the leg or foot is in bad relation to earth and ground, and the best thing to do is fly as the quickest means of escape from mortality. Would this indicate the figure of Philemon as totally detached from the mortal condition and hence more likely at home in the realm of Death, Hades, Satan & co, and which was the final destiny of Oedipous to wander in blindness in the chthonian womb of the maternal unconscious? Nevertheless, of course, why else would Jung call on the dead in his *Sermones ad Mortuous*, ostenasively located in Alexandria! Enter at once the realms of Macedonian Greeks such as Alexander and Aristotle and the daughter of that place, Cleopatra, and Ptolemaic Egypt of about 300 bc. Opens a realm of the dead that is part of a living history on its way to migrating to Iberia and then to the Medieval Germany favored by Jung. The Dead of Alexandria, however, has more to offer that would titillate Jung from the depth of his Hermetic being.

Act Two and enter the mystic Jewess and womb to Alchemy, Maria Prophetessa the Jewess who is credited with establishing the theoretical and practical foundations of alchemy, the forerunner of modern chemistry in the western world. She was one of the first chemists to combine the theories of alchemical science with the practical chemistry of the craft traditions. Although her theoretical contributions remained influential into the middle ages and beyond, Maria was more famous for her designs of laboratory apparatus. Although nothing is known of her life, there are many references to Maria in ancient texts and she is believed to have lived in Alexandria, Egypt, in the first century after. Alexandria, was founded by Alexander the Great in 332 BC, Under the ruler Ptolemy, Alexandria became the center of Greek science, featuring an institute of higher learning called the Museum, the Great Library, a zoo, botanical gardens and an observatory. However by the first century, the Greco- Roman world had entered an intellectual decline. Alchemy was the one science that continued to develop at a time when most scientists believed there was nothing new to discover and that all-important knowledge could be found in the works of the ancient Greeks.

Opus Mulierum: Women as the Pioneers of Alchemy

In the wake of the Alexandrian event, the Egyptian goddess Isis was said to be the founder of alchemy. However, in a greater antiquity the science was probably originated with the women who used the chemical processes of distillation, extraction, and sublimation to formulate perfumes and cosmetics in ancient Mesopotamia. Likewise, Babylonian women chemists used recipes and equipment derived from the kitchen. Thus, ancient alchemy was identified with women, and the work of the early alchemists occasionally was referred to as *opus mulierum*, or "women's work." Artists working with dyes and theories of color were also important sources for the practical aspects of Egyptian alchemy; but alchemical theory was steeped in the Gnostic tradition, centered in Alexandria. Gnosticism was a mixture of Jewish, Chaldean, and Egyptian mysticism, neo-platonism and later, Christianity. In alchemy, as in Gnosticism, the male and female elements were considered to be of equal importance.

Alchemy was a secretive science, perhaps to protect its practitioners from persecution; however, both the mystical cults and the crafts also had traditions of secrecy. In any case, it was common for alchemists to write under the name of a deity or famous person. Thus, Maria wrote under the name of Miriam the Prophetess, sister of Moses. In addition, she is referred to in alchemical literature as Maria the Jewess, Mary, Maria Prophetissa, and Maria the Sage, as well as Miriam. Maria's many alchemical treatises have been expanded, corrupted, and confused with other writings over the ages. However, fragments of her work, including one called the *Maria Practica*, are extant in ancient alchemical collections. She was quoted often by other early alchemists, particularly the Egyptian encyclopediast Zosimus (ca. 300). Maria the Jewess also may have been the author of "The Letter of the Crown and the Nature of the Creation by Mary the Copt of Egypt" which was found in a volume of Arabic alchemical manuscripts, translated from Greek. This work summarized the major theories of Alexandrian alchemy and described the manufacture of colored glass, as well as other chemical processes.

The ultimate goal of the alchemist was to transmute common metals into silver and gold, and who were scientists who were examining the nature of life and of chemical processes. Although their science was based in Aristotelian theory, they were the first true experimenters. Maria believed that metals were living males and females and that the products of her laboratory experiments were the result of sexual generation. The early alchemists believed that the base metals were evolving toward the perfect metal--gold--and they clearly distinguished between gilding or forming alloys of base metals to simulate gold and silver, and true transmutation. By transferring the "spirit" or vapor of gold to a base metal, as measured by the transfer of color, alchemists saw themselves as encouraging a natural process.

Maria invented, and improved on, techniques and tools that remain basic to laboratory science today and her writings described her designs for laboratory apparatus in great detail. Her water bath, the *balneum mariae* or "Maria's bath," was similar to a double-boiler and was used to maintain a constant temperature, or to slowly heat a substance. Two thousand years later, the water bath remains an essential component of the laboratory. In modern French, the double-boiler is called a *bain-marie.*

Distillation was essential to experimental alchemy and Maria invented a still or alembic and a three-armed still called the *tribikos.* The liquid to be distilled was heated in an earthenware vessel on a furnace. The vapor condensed in the ambix, which was cooled with sponges, and a rim on the inside of the ambix collected the distillate and carried it to three copper delivery spouts fitted with receiving vessels. Maria described how to make the copper tubing from sheet metal that was the thickness of a pastry pan. Flour paste was used to seal the joints.

Maria also studied the effects of arsenic, mercury, and sulfur vapors on metals, softening the metals and impregnating them with colors. For these experiments she invented the *kerotakis* process, her most important contribution to alchemical science. Her apparatus also came to be known as the kerotakis, a cylinder or sphere with a hemispherical cover, set on a fire. Suspended from the cover at the top of the cylinder was a triangular palette, used by artists to heat their mixtures of pigment and wax, and containing a copper-lead alloy or some other metal. Solutions of sulfur, mercury, or arsenic sulfide were heated in a pan near the bottom of the cylinder. The sulfur or mercury vapors condensed in the cover and the liquid condensate flowed back down, attacking the metal to yield a black sulfide called "Mary's Black ." This was believed to be the first step of transmutation. A sieve separated impurities from the black sulfide and continuous refluxing produced a gold-like alloy. Plant oils such as attar of roses also were extracted using the kerotakis.

Maria has been credited with inventing or improving upon the hot-ash bath and the dung-bed as laboratory heat sources and perfecting processes for producing phosphorescent gems. Maria's theoretical work included the concept of the macrocosm, or universe, and the microcosm, or individual body and she applied this concept to the processes of distillation and reflux.

By the third century, the alchemists of Alexandria were being persecuted and their texts were destroyed. Much of this work was rescued by the Arabs, who venerated Maria and adopted her alchemical theories. However, when alchemy was rediscovered in medieval Europe, it was primarily in the form of charlatanism. Laboratory chemistry advanced very little from the time of Maria to the mid-seventeenth century, nothstanding the efforts of St. Thomas Acquinas.

Jung and His Ghost Anima: Maria

Ah, would not Jung be united in a hierosgamous with this Jewess for her prognostic aphorism that was not only the alchemical formula but was to become the theoretic ground for all Jung's reckoning in his Analytical Psychology: *One becomes two, two becomes three and out of the third comes the one as the fourth.* The arrival of The One is, of course, the unus mundus of Gerhard Dorn. The German alchemist, and then Jung. Not so curiously, a Jewess stands as marker in Jung's psychological perspective. But here is a most cryptic love affair except for another femme inspiratrix in the figure of Jung's first patient, Sabina Speilrein. In her diary she notes: "Now- pair No. 4 [meaning she and Jung, ed.]. That is the present masculine pair [meaning Jung and his son born of Sabina, ed.]. The Christian in it my friend; he is a doctor, married. Other elements such as strong religious sense and the sense of calling, are things of which he possesses more than enough, for his father was a minister! At the time our poetry [their cryptic hyper transference "love affair," ed.], he had two girls , and the potentiality for a boy within him, which my unconscious ferreted out at the appropriate time in "prophetic dreams" [sired by the doctor as her Messiah\lover, ed.] He told me that he loved Jewish women that he wanted to love a dark Jewish girl. So in him, too, the urge to remain faithful to his religion and culture, as well as the drive to explore other possibilities through a new race, the drive to liberate himself from the paternal edicts through an unbelieving Jewess."[62] It is here that Jung likens to the Wandering Jew, doomed to life until the Second Coming and drawn in his fantasy as Philemon. No doubt Sabina served unmentionably as his Salome, his Jewess as Courtesan but not Madona, Miriam as more Magdalene than Virgin Mother..

From Foot to Phallus

Earth-form or Ka, thus become problematical for Jung since it touches him in his sensitive spot with regard to the practice of Art as recommended by his anima (Sabina). It is this a vast shadow area for him, a place of inferiority or lack of development of a specific function that is hardly real but, in the Narcissistic sense, an "eternal reflection." It is thus representative of Philemon's crippled leg, as well as that of Oedipus, "The cripple," notes Dr. Erel Shalit, "is the image of one who carries our complexes, as for instance Oedipus and Hephaestus do. By means of our complexes we become human, and our human potency derives from the complexes.

'While Oedipus is crippled, dragging along on his injured leg, the same awollen foot carries, as well, the potency of the erect penis.'"[63]

Dr. Shalit's metaphor is provocative since it also links the turgid nature of an erected penis as in cause to a crippling and which would certainly mollify Jung for what he attributed to the voice of "of a patient, a talented psychopath who had a strong transference to me. She had become a strong figure within my mind."[64] She would also be related to the Ka, as earth form and, as such, "reality principle" disturbing Jung in his closet practice of Art through his secret Red Book. Indeed, in more ways than one Sabina, the allegedly "psychopathic" patient\mistress of Jung wood be responsible for his 'swollen" nature by crippling his penis as La bella Juive is wont to do! The shadow aspect of such an image is early on anticipated by Jung by his baby dream of a giant rising up underground phallus that, as a chthonian apparition is non other than Hades qua the Devil itself and by which Thanatos and sexuality are consubstantially re-affirmed. However erotically preoccupied in the relationship, thanatos sets the pattern insofar as it drew Jung into his "Confrontation with the Unconscious," and the beginning of his reclaiming the elements of his No. 2 personality and its intimate relation with Chthonios and depth of the maternal unconscious.

The sins of the Garden thus persist but confined to that of Original Sin: that of sexual concupiscence. What may be called "The Final Sin," however, is left unjudged as the sin of knowing mortality and its predication as thanatos. Would that be the greatest evil of all: the awareness of death Yes, but only if it amounts to the sin of not resurrecting unto Eternal Life. Except for the arrival of Jesus Christ that sin remains unconsciously remote if not the one and openly greatest evil to visit the consciousness of humankind.

Accordingly, there is very little imagination left to accommodate the awareness of death except for quick resolution in the notion of a Hereafter which may be posited as either Life after Death or Eternal Death. In option for the latter, Jung proposed the unus mundus, as the one and only all encompassing World but which is the complement of the material world of the here and now and may, most literally ascribed as the "Other world:" The unus mundus, however, blunders into the Biblical World as the first day of creation and which is necessarily void or otherwise in a state of Lethe or oblivion, or must admit to the World as "nothing" or otherwise drawn by Aristotle as the necessary state of Nihilio as consubstancial with pure and unconditioned potential. Nevertheless, potential for what or as Fraulein Speilrein noted, "for New Being."

Being as new being, however, is a synonym for "other being" as would the unus mundus be for other world except we metaphysically marry paradox and metaphor. The question remains rhetorically tautological and thus reasonably impossible in its metaphysical venue. Not so, however if it means to fall back to Jung's fantasy answer in his Septem Sermones ad Mortuous where "The dead came back from Jerusalem, where they found not what they sought. They prayed me let them in and besought my word, and thus I began my teaching" not, however as Jung, but his hyper-Ego as Philomen in voice as Basilides, the Gnostic seer. In addition, where must this seer be found but "in Alexandria, the city where the East toucheth the West" and Persia bonded in marriage with the |Hellenic realm to produce a child that continues to evolve and mature as Western Civilization except for the collective Western anima as **La femme Fatal.**

In an historical perspective, this is in kind to the mimimalizing of the importance of Alexander's arrival in Egypt, complete with Ptolemian Dynasties and a succession of the Macedonian Cleopatras, the original of whom was the sister of Alexander and all the way forward by a succession of Cleopatras galore to Caesar, Mark Anthony and the Arrival of the God-man Soter of Resurrection. It all Led me wonder that Mary Magdalene was a Cleopatra in disguise washing the feet of her Savior and lover. She, however, had a mythogenic antecedent; Persephone *Parthenos* abducted by Hades, Lord of Death to become the Queen of Death. Jesus and his brother as the devil are thus indulged by a common anima. It is at this point of reminiscing that some serious concern is registered if at all one is so inclined to pick the mushrooms grown in the garden of archetypes which is only a block and a half away from the Garden of Eden and a deck above where Lady Eve emerges as the Bride and Queen of Death, however, enforced as consort of the Lord Hades. Why not, then, here recall Lady Persephone, once virgin daughter of mother goddess Demeter, or Ge-Meter, of this Earth, nevermind that below the topos of Mother Earth is Chthonios, the realm of Death and its Lord variously known as Hades but in mythogenic Truth, a Zeus below the belt, doubled as Satan or the Devil except in more polite Greek terms, as *Zeus katacthonios* that represents the divine and mighty Saturnian genital of the celestial Zeus above. Alternatively, right to the Point Death and its emblem as a rising Phallus. But here is mirrored precisely the chronic duplex personality of the optimum male as the archetypal mushroom that is both edible and toxic of his duplex, if only split, personality.

The mistress here is the *Femme Fatal Royale*, the epitome of anima and no less the mistress as Lady of Death. Leonardo called and painted her as his Mona Lisa whose sardonic smile gave her away as a Lady of infinite and fatal intrigue and in the thrall of her Lord master Hades or Death. Beneath her skin, like my ship, stirred a Teutonic hell borer. "Ho, Sire would you entertain the lady with your soul-sucking the better for Hero to know Death?" Nevertheless, of course, that is what such ecstasy is all about: to tempt Death before and after now, where the past and the future conjoin as life lost and inestimable pure potential refound. Nevertheless, for an old gent such as myself, after a wife and kids and followed by young mistresses, I am still obliged to soul-suck the Grand Dame who as both Death and the The Past, I now call Mother Israel. Indeed, the Jews have been indulging their Swan song for three thousand years! Why not I who first noticed the possibility when my ship, no less named "The Alexander" exploded at sea but, like myself, refused to sink because it had not struck an explosive vagrant sea-going mine, as the US Army claimed, but a bomb placed in the ship by the still at war remnants of the defeated Third Reich. But there you see not only the duplexity of my Flying Dutchman, The USAT E. B. Alexander, but of Alexandria "where the East meets the West the better to ease my Illyerian soul-lady.

FINIS

ENDNOTES

1. MDR., p.87. ADVANCE \d12
2. *MDR., p.87.*
3. *Ibid.*
4. *psychology of the Trinity*
5. *(Jung, Memories, Dreams, Reflections, p. 183).*
6. *MDR, p. 45.*
7. *Memories, Dreams, Reflections, by C.G.Jung and Aniela Jaffeee, Chap. VI*
8. *MDR., p.13.*
9. *Mysterium, p. 341-2.*
10. *MDR., p.285.*
11. *Directed by Abel Gance, Produced by Charles PathΘ, Written by Abel Gance.Editing by AndrΘe Danis, Release date(s) 25 April 1919 (France),24 May 1920 (UK), 9 October 1921 (USA), Running time 166 min. (2008 restoration), Country France, Language Silent French intertitles. Cited in Wikipedia, the free encyclopedia.*
12. *Reference:Kevin,_Brownlow,1968, p.533.*
13. *Psychology and alchemy: C.W. 12, par. 8, pge. 8.*
14. *Santiago Zabala (ed.), Weakening Philosophy: Essays in Honour of Gianni Vattimo, McGill-Queen's University Press.*
15. The Gnostic Religion: Beacon Press, Boston, p.134.
16. *Psychological types or The Psychology of Ondividuation*, Pantheon Books, *Definitions*, p.611.
17. Ibid, p.612
18. *Parmenides,* Indiana University Press, p.138.
19. Ibid, p.138.
20. Ibid, p. 138.
21. Ibid., p.138.
22. Prof. E.E. Peters: *Greek Philosophical Terms*, New York University Press, p.92.
23. Civilization in Transition, bollingen Series XX, par. 374.
24. Mysterium, p.188.

25. Dr. Marie-Louse von Franze: *Aurora Consurgens*, Inner City Books, p.396, fn.,178.
26. Ibid., p.189.
27. Jung's *Mysterium conniunctionus*, pp.533.
28. Ibid,.p.533.
29. Mysterium: p.271.
30. Ibid, p. 535.
31. *Energeia and Entelecheia "Act" in Aristotle*, by George A. Blair, Iniversity of Ottawa Press, p.17
32. Mysterium: p.243.
33. Mysterium, p.64.
34. Mysterium, p.190 fn.
35. Dr. Monika wikman: *Pregnant Darkness*. Berwick, Maine: Nicolas-Hays, Inc., 2004. Page 59.
36. May 16, 2012, p. 210.
37. Ibid, p.535.
38. Mysterius,p. 534.
39 MDR, p.175.
40. MDR., p. 185.
41. John Burnet, *Early Greek Philosophy*, Herakleitos of Ephesus (fragment 127).
42. *Memories, Dreams, Reflextions*, Vintage Books, p.87.
43. ibid. p. 87.
44. *Civilization in Transition*, Bollingen Series XX, (par. 499).
45. MDR, p.270.
46. Jung; A Biogrphy, by Dierdre Bair, Back Bay Books, p.364.
47. *The Masculne Mysteries*, Author House, 2005.
48 AURORA CONSURGENS: A document Attributed to Thomas Acquinas On the Problem of Opposites in alchemy, inner City Books, toronto, Canada,p. 399.
49. *Civilization in Transition*, Bollingen Series XX, par. 374).
50. MDR., p.225.
51. *The Jewish Woman in Christian Literature Madona or coutesan?*, the Seabury Press (1982, pgs.6-7.
52. Originally published in *The Undiscovered Self* (1957) and included in the Collected Works as *Civilization in Transition*, Bollingen Series XX, par. 499. Pars. 500, et al par.504.
53. *Alchemical Studies*, par. 246.
54. *Psychology and Religion*, CW 11, 600, n. 13].

55. Mysterium, p. 428.

56. Ibid, ps. 373-4.

57. MDR, p. 185-6.

58. Martin Heidwgger: *Parmenides*, Indiana Univerity Press, Bloomingtonand Minneapolis, pgs. 4-5.

59. From Wikipedia, the free encyclopedia.

60. From Aldo Carotenuto?s A Secret Symetry, Pantheon Books, p. 40.

61. Livia Bitton-Jackson, *Madona or Courtesan: The Jewish Woman in ChristianLiterature,* The Seabury Press/NY. P. 3.

62. From Aldo Carotenuto's *A Secret Symetry,* Pantheon Books, p. 40

63. Enemy Cripple & Bedggar: shadow in the Hero's Path, by Erel Shalit. Dr.Shalit, an acquaintance of mine, is an Analyhtical Psychologist pracicing in Israel.

64. MDR, p. 185.

INDEX

ABOUT THE AUTHOR:

Bernard X. Bovasso is essentially a painter, a poet and a onetime art and drama reviewer for the Woodstock Times of Woodstock, N.Y. His interest in the work of C.G. Jung of Zurich goes back to his student days at the Cooper Union Art School where upon graduation he was awarded a fellowship to study at the Yale Univeristy Summer School of Fine Art (1948-51). Prior to that he attended the NY City High School of Music and Art. Upon graduation and during WWII he enlisted in the U.S. Maritime Training Service and then on active duty in the U.S. Merchant Marine at the close of World War II (1945 to 1949). In September of 1946 he was signed aboard the USAT E.B. Alexander, a US Army troopship when it exploded in the North Sea and ordered abandoned. He was awareded a US Coast Guard Honorable Discharge for service in the US Merchant Marine and another such discharge from the US Army for service with the US Army Sea Transport Service. For service in a war zone he was assignerd combat status by the Veterans Administration.. After release from service he often found it necessary to take a sea voyage during college summer recess to support himself at school. During the summer of '51 he was assigned to an LST loaded with giant snow plows and headed for Thule, Greenland for the construction of the early warning base just 500 miles south of the North Pole. Operation Blue Jay, as the mission was called, was composed of U.S. Army supply ships in the company of a U.S. Navy task force that included an aircraft carrier. Pres. Truman was worried the USSR might try to intercept the mission and the carrier TBF planes were armed with depth charges if Russian U-boats made an appearance.The trip cured him of ever going to sea again. But he was also cured of Academia when, after Cooper Union, he turned down a fellowship to the Yale University Art School. He was perhaps much influenced by Herman Melville's claim: "The whale ship was my Harvard and Yale." Soon after he was in analysis with Freida a Stern of NY City, a protegé of Toni Wolff of Zurich who was a close colleague of C. G. Jung.. After that his interest in the Analytical Psychology became intensive and eventually led to a study of philosophy. At the New School for Social Research in NYC, he studied pre-Socratic Philosophy with Prof. Hans Jonas, known for his book on Gnosticism, and Ernest Cassirer's Philosophy of Symbolic Forms with Prof. Eugen Gadol (1963). During 2005 his book, The Masculine Mysteries followed by The Polyimagical Realm, A Critique of Dr. James Hillman's Polytheistic Archetypal Psychology wers published. This was followed by his Animus Rising, a study of the feminine influence in American culture, all published by Author House of Bloomington IN..

www.ingramcontent.com/pod-product-compliance
Lightning Source LLC
Chambersburg PA
CBHW020439290526
45785CB00002B/920